105

A Voice from the Vietnam War

Recent Title in
Voices of Twentieth-Century Conflict

A Voice from the Holocaust
Eve Nussbaum Soumerai and Carol D. Schulz

A Voice from the Vietnam War

Russell H. Coward, Jr.

Voices of Twentieth-Century Conflict
Carol Schulz, Series Editor

Greenwood Press
Westport, Connecticut • London

Library of Congress Cataloging-in-Publication Data

Coward, Russell, 1946-
   A voice from the Vietnam War / by Russell H. Coward, Jr.
      p.   cm. — (Voices of twentieth century conflict)
   Includes bibliographical references and index.
   ISBN 0–313–32586–3 (alk. paper)
   1. Coward, Russell, 1946–   2. Vietnamese Conflict, 1961–1975—Personal
narratives, American.   3. Vietnam—History.   I. Title.   II. Series.
DS559.5.C685   2004
959.704'34'092—dc22   2004047482
   [B]

British Library Cataloguing in Publication Data is available.

Library of Congress Catalog Card Number: 2004047482
ISBN: 0–313–32586–3

First published in 2004

Greenwood Press, 88 Post Road West, Westport, CT 06881
An imprint of Greenwood Publishing Group, Inc.
www.greenwood.com

Printed in the United States of America

The paper used in this book complies with the
Permanent Paper Standard issued by the National
Information Standards Organization (Z39.48–1984).

10 9 8 7 6 5 4 3 2 1

Contents

Contents

Contents

Foreword

What Americans call the "Vietnam War" is referred to by the Vietnamese as the "American War." To the Vietnamese, it was the final struggle in their 2,000-year battle for freedom from foreign domination. To the Americans, it was a critical Cold War confrontation between democracy and communism.

This narrative alternately presents the history of Vietnam and the development of the author's awareness and understanding of American involvement there. Russell Coward's sensitivity to the perspectives of Americans and Vietnamese not only clarifies the issues surrounding the war, but also increases readers' understanding of the reasons for the intense conflicts in both countries.

He takes readers on a journey from his childhood and his own father's traditionally patriotic view of the world, through his adolescence during the Cold War and into his early adulthood when he received his U.S. Air Force orders to teach English in Saigon. Readers will witness the events of his youth and their effects on his developing attitude toward the war.

By the end of the war, thousands of Americans and hundreds of thousands of Vietnamese had lost their lives. Many more on both sides had been severely wounded or maimed. In the United Sates, millions had watched the war on television and argued about its significance. Many had demonstrated their support of America's role in Vietnam, and many had demonstrated their opposition to it.

Three decades later, with American soldiers again in combat in foreign lands, we are still debating the meaning of our involvement in Vietnam. And rightly so. *A Voice from the Vietnam War* is an excellent resource for students studying either the past or the present foreign policies and resulting military engagements.

Carol Schulz
Series Editor, Voices of Twentieth-Century Conflict

Acknowledgments

I wish to thank my editor, Carol Schulz, for offering me the opportunity to write about the year I spent teaching English in Saigon and learning about Vietnam, the United States, and myself. Her comments on my drafts were perceptive and helpful.

I also thank Sarah Colwell at Greenwood Press for her patience while I tried to figure out a way to organize the historical material and my personal experience. Her input helped prevent me from lapsing into overly conversational tone and diction.

Throughout the over two years of intermittent writing and revising, my wife Tuoi and my sons Russell and Adam were both editorially helpful and personally sustaining. Tuoi provided technical and editorial support, coffee, and snacks, Russell read drafts during his summer vacation, and Adam read drafts and worked wonders restoring pictures that had been boxed in our basement for years.

Introduction

I was born on June 30, 1946, to Russell H. Coward, former Lieutenant in the U.S. Army Air Corps and Anna Grace Coward. Mom had waited to marry Dad until after he returned safely from World War II. Their wedding picture stood on the mantle above the fireplace in our living room. Mom was smiling in a long, white, silk dress, and Dad was beaming in his army dress uniform. He had been a soldier, but I knew that I would never be one.

Not that I was a natural-born pacifist. My favorite Christmas present ever was a two-holster set of Roy Rogers pistols. I spent the day shooting cousins, aunts, uncles, and Mom and Dad. I also loved to play with toy soldiers, trucks, jeeps, tanks, and artillery. During the summers in the 1950s in suburban Rochester, New York, my friends and I climbed trees, dug foxholes, and played war games down in Corbett's Glen. We proudly wore our fathers' army belts, drank Kool-Aid from their canteens, and pretended to eat dinner from their mess kits.

Soon, however, our childhood fascination with playing war was replaced by our adolescent obsession with sports. We started playing baseball as soon as the snow melted in the spring, and Little League games lasted through the summer. In the fall, we played soccer at school and football on the weekends. And in the winter, we played basketball at school and outdoors, even if we had to shovel off the court.

**Author's parents, Anna Grace Wilson and Lt. Russell
H. Coward, on their wedding day, June 3, 1944.**

I also liked to read books. So I got A's on my early report cards.
But I preferred sports even though I didn't get out of the minors
in Little League until I was eleven years old, and was usually
picked last when teams were chosen for neighborhood football
games. I was small and short, but I loved basketball and practiced
enough to eventually make the high school varsity.

In the fall of 1964, I went off to Trinity College in Hartford,
Connecticut, to continue reading and playing basketball. I would
have gone to the University of Michigan like my father had, but
I knew that I could never play basketball at that NCAA Division
I powerhouse. At Trinity, I majored in English, made the Division
III basketball team, and graduated in 1968.

A year later, I found myself in a U.S. Air Force uniform at
Travis Air Force Base outside of San Francisco, waiting to board
a plane for Vietnam. At the time, I knew little about Vietnam. But

Author with Roy Rogers pistols in living room on Dale Road on Christmas Day, 1954.

during my year living in Saigon and teaching English to South Vietnamese officers, I learned a lot about that small, ancient Eastern country. I learned a lot about America, that tall, broad-shouldered, young Western power, too.

Timeline

1885	France forms French Indochina, including Vietnam, Laos, and Cambodia.
1930	Ho Chi Minh organizes the Indochinese Communist Party.
1941	
May	Ho Chi Minh leads the formation of Vietnam Doc-Lap Dong-Minh Hoi—The League for the Independence of Vietnam—the Viet Minh.
1945	
September 2	Ho Chi Minh declares the independence of the Democratic Republic of Vietnam (DRV) and forms the People's Army of Vietnam (PAVN), led by General Vo Nguyen Giap.
October	35,000 French soldiers arrive in Vietnam to restore French rule.
1946	
December 19	Viet Minh attack the French in Hanoi, beginning the First Indochina War.

1950

| February | McCarthyism erupts in the United States. |

| June 30 | President Harry S. Truman orders ground troops into Korea. |

| July 26 | Truman initiates military aid to the French in Vietnam with $15 million. |

1952

| November | Dwight D. Eisenhower, former Allied commander in Europe in World War II, is elected the 34th President of the United States. |

1953

| July 23 | The Korean War ends as an armistice divides the country at the 38th parallel into the communist-controlled Democratic People's Republic of Korea (North Korea) and the Republic of Korea (South Korea). |

| November | France fortifies its air base at Dien Bien Phu in northwest Vietnam, and General Vo Nguyen Giap masses Viet Minh troops and artillery in the surrounding area. |

1954

| March 15 | Siege of Dien Bien Phu begins. |

| May 7 | French surrender at Dien Bien Phu. |

| May 8 | The Geneva Conference on Indochina begins with the United States, England, China, the Soviet Union, France, Cambodia, Laos, and Vietnam (represented by the Viet Minh and Bao Dai, the French-appointed emperor). |

July 21	The Geneva Accords divide Vietnam at the 17th parallel, granting Ho Chi Minh and the Viet Minh control of the Democratic Republic of Vietnam (North Vietnam) and Bao Dai's regime control of southern Vietnam. The Accords also provide for elections to be held in 1956 to reunify the country.
October	Bao Dai installs Ngo Dinh Diem as his Prime Minister.

1955

January	U.S. military aid to South Vietnam begins.
October 23	Diem ousts Bao Dai, and proclaims himself the first president of the Republic of South Vietnam

1956 Elections scheduled by the Geneva Accords are not held.

1960

November	John F. Kennedy is elected the 35th president of the United States.
December 20	The National Front for the Liberation of South Vietnam (NLF; later the Viet Cong) is formed, beginning the Second Indochina War.

1962

February 6	The United States Military Assistance Command for Vietnam (MACV) is formed.

1963

November 2	President Ngo Dinh Diem and his brother Ngo Dinh Nhu are assassinated in a military coup.
November 22	President Kennedy is assassinated.

1964

August 7   Congress passes the Gulf of Tonkin Resolution.

November 3   President Lyndon B. Johnson is elected with 61 percent of the popular vote, the biggest margin in U.S. history.

1965

March 2   Operation Rolling Thunder—the bombing of North Vietnam—begins.

March 8   First American combat troops, 3,500 Marines, arrive in Vietnam to defend the air base at Da Nang; offensive operations are kept secret from the press and the public for two months.

April 17   15,000 students demonstrate in Washington to protest Rolling Thunder.

June 18   Nguyen Van Thieu and Nguyen Cao Ky take control of the government in South Vietnam— the tenth government in less than two years.

October 16   Antiwar rallies occur in numerous cities in the United States and around the world.

October 30   Five Medal of Honor recipients lead a march in Washington in support of American involvement in Vietnam.

November 27   Antiwar protestors circle the White House and then march on to the Washington Monument.

1966

March 1   Senator Wayne Morse of Oregon leads an attempt to repeal the Gulf of Tonkin Resolution that is defeated in the Senate 92–5.

June 4	*The New York Times* prints a three-page antiwar advertisement signed by 6,400 teachers and professors.

1967

January 23	Senator J. William Fullbright publishes *The Arrogance of Power*, a book that is critical of American policy in Vietnam.
February 8–10	American religious groups lead a nationwide "Fast for Peace."
April 14	Former Vice President Nixon (under Eisenhower) asserts that the antiwar protests are "prolonging the war."
April 24	General William Westmoreland condemns antiwar demonstrators for aiding the enemy.
May 13	A demonstration in New York is held to support the war.
October 21–23	March on the Pentagon is conducted by antiwar protestors.
November 29	Secretary of Defense Robert McNamara resigns, following other top Johnson aides McGeorge Bundy, George Ball, and Bill Moyers.

1968

January–February	Tet Offensive
March 16	My Lai: U.S. Army soldiers kill Vietnamese civilians in an airborne assault against suspected Viet Cong encampments. (Incident is covered up for a year.)
April 4	Dr. Martin Luther King Jr. is assassinated.

April	Antiwar demonstrators seize five buildings at Columbia University, and 200,000 students across the United States refuse to attend classes.
May 10	Peace talks begin in Paris.
June 5	Senator Robert Kennedy is assassinated immediately following his victory in California's Democratic presidential primary.
November 5	Richard Nixon narrowly defeats Hubert Humphrey to become the 37th U.S. President, and later in the month names Harvard professor Henry Kissinger as his National Security Advisor.

1969

March	News of My Lai becomes public.
March 17	Nixon authorizes Operation Menu, the secret bombing of Cambodia.
June 8	In a meeting with President Thieu on Midway Island, President Nixon announces the "Vietnamization" of the war and the first U.S. troop withdrawal of 25,000.
September 2	Ho Chi Minh dies at seventy-nine.
October 15	National Moratorium Day.
November 15	Mobilization in Washington draws 250,000, the largest antiwar protest in U.S. history.
December 1	The first draft lottery since World War II is held.

1970

April 30	President Nixon announces the sending of troops into Cambodia.
May 2	American college students protest the invasion of Cambodia.

May 4	At Kent State University in Ohio, National Guardsmen kill four student protestors and wound nine.
May	Over four hundred colleges and universities across the nation close.
June 24	U.S. Senate repeals the Gulf of Tonkin Resolution.
December 22	Congress forbids the use of ground troops in Cambodia or Laos.

1971

March 29	Lieutenant William Calley is found guilty of the murder of civilians in My Lai.
April 19	Vietnam Veterans Against the War begin a week of nationwide protests.
May 3–5	12,000 antiwar protestors are arrested in Washington.
June 13	*The New York Times* publishes the Pentagon Papers.
June 18	*The Washington Post* publishes the Pentagon Papers.
June 30	In response to President Nixon's attempt to block publication of the Pentagon Papers, the U.S. Supreme Court rules in favor of the *Times* and the *Post*.
September 22	Captain Ernest Medina is acquitted of all charges concerning the killing of civilians at My Lai.

1972

April 15–20   Americans protest the bombing of North Vietnam and the mining of Haiphong harbor.

June 17   Five burglars are arrested inside Democratic Committee offices in the Watergate building in Washington, D.C.

November 7   President Nixon defeats Senator George McGovern, whose platform stressed "immediate and complete withdrawal from Vietnam," by the biggest margin in U.S. history.

1973

January 27   The Paris Peace Accords are signed by representatives of the United States, North Vietnam, and South Vietnam.

March 29   Last American combat troops leave Vietnam.

November 7   Congress passes the War Powers Resolution requiring the President to acquire the support of Congress within ninety days of sending American troops abroad.

1974

May 9   Congress initiates impeachment proceedings against President Nixon as a result of Watergate.

August 9   President Nixon resigns.

September 16   President Gerald Ford announces a clemency program for draft evaders and military deserters.

1975

March–April	The North Vietnamese Army crosses the demilitarized zone (DMZ), beginning the "Ho Chi Minh Campaign," its march south to Saigon.
April 21	South Vietnam President Thieu resigns and is taken to Taiwan by CIA personnel.
April 30	The last Americans leave Saigon at 8:30 in the morning. Three hours later, North Vietnamese tanks knock down the fence at the Presidential Palace and proclaim the reunification of Vietnam.

1976   American Bicentennial celebration.

1977   Vietnam is admitted to the United Nations.

1982

November 13	Dedication of the Vietnam Veterans Memorial (VVM; also "the Wall").

1995   The United States and Vietnam restore diplomatic relations.

Part I

A Ticket to Saigon (1946–1969)

History of Vietnam through World War II

Vietnam's origins lie hidden in mythology and archaeology. According to myth, the Vietnamese people are the descendents of the one hundred offspring of a dragon and a goddess. Fifty of the children went with their mother, the goddess, into the mountains, and the other fifty went with their father, the dragon, to the seaside.

Archaeology has established Vietnam's roots in the Bronze Age, and recorded history notes that Vietnam was conquered by China in 111 B.C. Chinese rule lasted for over a thousand years. There followed nine centuries of independence, disrupted internally by recurring dynastic rivalries and externally by frequent foreign invaders.

During the Age of Imperialism, French missionaries moved into Southeast Asia. Troops soon followed. In the French Indochina War (1882–1883), the French wrested control of Vietnam from China and subsequently established a protectorate that included Vietnam and Cambodia. In 1893, Laos was added. A French newsreel from the early 1900s described the effects concisely: "In regions of hostility and misery, French civilization has brought peace, work, prosperity and joy."

In the introduction to *Requiem*, an anthology of photographs taken by photographers who were killed while covering the wars in Vietnam, the effects are described quite differently by co-editor Tim Page. "The French undermined Indochina's social system for the sake of profit. Rubber-plantation workers were little more than slaves; indentured peasant farmers couldn't feed their families because their bumper rice crops were being exported for cash."

Educated by the French, but with genuine concern for the peasant farmers, the man who would organize and lead Vietnam's drive for independence was born in 1890 in central Vietnam.

Nguyen Tat Thanh learned the French values of *Liberté, Égalité, Fraternité* (Liberty, Equality, Fraternity—the battle cry of the French Revolution) in school, but outside of school, he experienced the daily oppression of his family and his countrymen. His father was a mandarin who was dismissed by the French for his criticism of their domination of the Vietnamese people.

In 1908, Thanh was expelled from the French school in Hue for his rebellious activities. He translated a peasant petition demanding lower taxes for peasant farmers from Vietnamese into French. Three years later, he took a job as a cook on a French ocean liner and left his homeland. He worked in the United States and England before settling in Paris in 1917 and changing his name to Nguyen Ai Quoc, "Nguyen the Patriot." During his days in Boston and New York, he was amazed by the fact that immigrants in America had more rights than Vietnamese in Vietnam. In Paris, reading Vladimir Lenin's theses on nationalism and colonialism, he began to change his goals. His initial commitment to winning greater rights for the Vietnamese people in French Indochina evolved into a commitment to winning independence for Vietnam.

In Paris at the Versailles Conference following World War I, he sought admission to speak for recognition of Vietnam, but he was turned away. Soon thereafter, he became a founding member of the French Communist Party. He traveled back and forth often between Moscow and southern China prior to his return to Vietnam in 1941 as Ho Chi Minh, "He who enlightens." Soon he and General Vo Nguyen Giap formed Vietnam Doc-Lap Dong-Minh Hoi (The League for the Independence of Vietnam)—the Viet Minh—a nationalist coalition founded upon traditional Vietnamese values and Lenin's commitment to self-determination, and empowered by Vietnam's 5,000-year-old fear and hatred of foreign dominance.

At the same time, the People's Army of Vietnam (PAVN) was formed under General Giap. His first force was a mere thirty-four soldiers with an arsenal of two Colt pistols and one Thompson submachine gun. Giap had barely escaped the French in 1939.

Following his flight from Hanoi into southern China, his wife was arrested and imprisoned, and she died. Accounts differ over whether she was beaten to death or committed suicide. Giap's sister was also arrested and she was executed. Other key Viet Minh leaders included Pham Van Dong and Le Duc Tho. Dong survived two four-year terms in French prisons. "The prisons were our schools," he later explained as President of a unified Vietnam in 1975. Tho eventually led the National Liberation Front (Viet Cong) and served as special advisor to the North Vietnamese delegation at the Paris Peace Conferences from 1968–1973.

During the early years of World War II, Japan had taken control of most of eastern Asia. Japanese troops moved into northern Vietnam in 1940 and took complete control of Vietnam a year later by an agreement with the Vichy government of German-occupied France.

Prior to the Japanese attack on Pearl Harbor, President Franklin Roosevelt had been opposed to France's return to rule in Indochina. He met with Prime Minister Winston Churchill of England at sea in August of 1941, and the two formulated the Atlantic Charter. Its third principle "for a better future world" was "respect [for] the right of all peoples to choose the form of government under which they will live and wish to see sovereign rights and self government restored to those who have been forcibly deprived of them." The Atlantic Charter later became the basis for the United Nations Charter.

Freedom and autonomy were also the Viet Minh's main goals. The group's first political action followed a devastating famine in northern Vietnam in 1944–1945 that caused approximately 2 million deaths, 25 percent of the region's population. While Vietnamese people were dying of starvation, Vietnamese rice was being exported to Japan and France. Led by the Viet Minh, peasants seized the rice stocks in Hanoi. The narrator of PBS's *Vietnam: A Television History* series, asserts, "This gave the Viet Minh a political edge that they never lost."

During the later stages of World War II, the Viet Minh and the Office of Strategic Services (OSS, precursor of the CIA) became

Viet Minh leaders and OSS officers. Ho Chi Minh, in white shirt, second from right. Probably late 1944 or early 1945.

temporary allies. Seven OSS officers were sent into southern China to rescue American pilots and harass the Japanese. Ho Chi Minh rescued a downed American pilot and delivered him to the OSS.

One OSS officer recalls Ho as primarily a nationalist and secondarily a communist. Ho's predominant concern was for the welfare of the Vietnamese people, not the dissemination of an international political ideology. In 1958 he wrote, "Socialism is everyone working together to provide food to eat, clothes to wear and homes to live in." During this temporary alliance between the United States and the Viet Minh, OSS officers trained General Giap's top 200 troops, who became the leaders in wars against first France and then the United States.

Following the surrender of Japan and the end of World War II, France sought to reestablish its colonial control of Vietnam, but the Viet Minh were determined to secure their country's independence. Their goal was partially rooted in the American history lessons taught to them by Ho Chi Minh, the first Vietnamese teacher of American history. On September 2, 1945, in Hanoi, Ho Chi Minh officially proclaimed the independence of the Democratic Republic of Vietnam, stating:

> All men are created equal; they are endowed by the Creator with certain unalienable rights; among them are Life, Liberty and the Pursuit of happiness.
>
> This immortal statement was made in the Declaration of Independence of the United States of America in 1776. In a broader sense this means: All the peoples on earth are equal from birth, all the peoples have a right to life, to be happy and free.

A year after its formation, Giap's PAVN had acquired 35,000 pistols and rifles, over 1,000 submachine guns, and 54 heavy artillery guns that it captured during initial skirmishes with French troops. But the Viet Minh alliance with the United States was short-lived. America was being asked by France to aid the reestablishment of its dominance in Indochina. At the end of World War II there was a clear division of opinion regarding Vietnam in the U.S. State Department. The European division supported France, but the Far Eastern Division, which was well aware of the tremendous surge of nationalism in Southeast Asia, was leery of supporting French colonialism. As a result, the United States had no official policy regarding Indochina.

This lack of a clear policy in Washington was further hampered by pervasive misunderstanding of Ho Chi Minh and his status in the eyes of all Vietnamese. U.S. governmental officials perceived him as first and foremost a communist, while his people revered him first and foremost as a nationalist. Republican Senator Thurston Morton realized this discrepancy. In Emile de Antonio's film *Vietnam: In the Year of the Pig*, Morton says, "The first thing that we failed to recognize was that Ho Chi Minh, communist or whatnot, was considered by the people of Vietnam as the George Washington of his country. Whether we liked him or not, whether we liked his particular economic or social system, we needed to remember that he was indeed considered by people in South Vietnam and North Vietnam as the George Washington of his country."

In late 1945, OSS Major A. Peter Dewey, while in Saigon looking for Allied POWs, commented, "Indochina is burning, the French and British are finished here, and we ought to clear out of Southeast Asia." On September 26, 1945, Dewey was killed outside of Saigon. Both the French and the Viet Minh blamed each other. Sources disagree about whether his death was a political assassination or merely an accident, but Major A. Peter Dewey was the first American killed in Vietnam. World War II was over, but the struggle for independence was just beginning in Vietnam, and what journalist Walter Lippman called "the cold war" was just beginning in America.

Dale Road

When my Dad got out of the Army, he traded his uniform for a suit and tie and worked in Buffalo, New York, for five years before moving to Rochester to work for his father-in-law at Wilson's Royal Tire. We moved into a new house on a new street in the suburbs, just like millions of other American families.

Every morning between 7:00 and 7:30, Mr. Burrell, Mr. Leonard, Mr. Mear, Mr. Jacobstein, Mr. Ellis, and my Dad kissed their missuses good-bye, backed their Fords and Chevys out of their driveways, and drove off to their jobs in Rochester. Every morning from September through June, Mrs. Burrell, Mrs. Leonard, Mrs. Mear, Mrs. Jacobstein, Mrs. Ellis, and my Mom made sure that their children finished their breakfasts, put their jackets on, had their books and notebooks, and got outside to the bus stop on Dale Road.

Susie Burrell, Dickie Leonard, Karen Mear, Dave Jacobstein, David Ellis, and I did not realize that our neighborhood and our lives were not exactly like the neighborhoods and lives of every other kid in the world. We carried the sandwiches that our mothers made in our little metal Mickey Mouse lunch boxes. We tried to do our work in school. We cooperated when our school had air raid drills and our teachers told us to crouch under our desks. And we learned that communism was bad and that Russia (not the U.S.S.R.) wanted to take over the world.

We knew that America had just won World War II. Every Fourth of July, we celebrated winning our independence from England almost 200 years earlier, but we did not know that other people in other countries were fighting for their independence while we were learning to read and write and ride bicycles and hit baseballs.

By the summer of 1954, I had discarded my tricycle and was

proudly pedaling a Schwinn two-wheeler around the neighbor-hood. I had traded in my Hopalong Cassidy outfit for a Little League uniform. I was reading Tom and Jerry, Donald Duck, and Superman comic books, Hardy Boys mysteries, and the comics and sports pages of Rochester's morning and afternoon newspapers.

By the summer of 1954, the Vietnamese, led by General Giap, had defeated the French to end the First Indochina War and secure the independence proclaimed by Ho Chi Minh nine years earlier. It had not been easy.

The First Indochina War

At the Potsdam Conference following the end of World War II, the victorious Allies decided that Chinese troops would supervise the departure of Japanese soldiers from northern Vietnam and British troops would supervise the Japanese departure from southern Vietnam. After confiscating Japanese weapons, however, the British troops turned them over to the French, who were intent on reestablishing their colonial rule. The French were supremely confident that their greater military force would prevail over the Viet Minh's smaller and less well-equipped PAVN.

But the will of the Viet Minh was strong. "We may lose ten Vietnamese for every one French soldier, but in the end we will win," vowed Ho Chi Minh, as reported in PBS's *Vietnam: A Television History.*

"We are ready," echoed PAVN commander Giap.

On December 19, 1946, fifteen months after Ho Chi Minh had proclaimed Vietnamese independence, a force of 30,000 Viet Minh attacked French troops in Hanoi, beginning the First Indochina War. Commanding General Giap announced, "Our resistance will be long and arduous, but our cause is just and we will surely triumph."

France's commanding General Etienne Vallery countered, "If they want a fight, they'll get it."

Disturbed by communist uprisings in China and Korea, and apprehensive about being labeled soft on communism, President Harry Truman pledged American support to the French.

Initially, the French named Bao Dai Emperor of Vietnam, but the Vietnamese knew that he was merely a puppet of the colonial power. In 1950, disturbed by the persistence of Giap's forces and the growing unrest over increasing French casualties, France announced *Le Jeunnissement*, "The Yellowing" of the war. In an effort to increase Bao Dai's credibility and reduce French casualties, the French formed and trained a national army of southern Vietnamese to bolster Dai's power.

America's aid to France increased and by 1953 the United States was paying 80 percent of the costs of the war. Despite American support and French control of the cities and the daylight hours, the Viet Minh still controlled the countryside and the nights. France focused on its base at Dien Bein Phu in the north, and built up its troops and munitions there. They deemed the base "untouchable," confident that Giap could not move his troops, supplies, and artillery over the mountainous terrain into threatening positions.

But 51,000 Viet Minh carried supplies on their backs and bicycles, and dragged their artillery up the steep mountainsides. Once his troops were in position, Giap struck quickly. On March 13, 1954, an assault comparable to the Allied D-Day attack began. On March 14, the base's airstrip was destroyed and the French artillery commander committed suicide. By nightfall the following day, the Viet Minh controlled the perimeter. Then Giap changed his strategy. He had his troops dig trenches and tunnels, and settle in for a lengthy siege.

In late March, a desperate France requested more support from Washington. American military leaders considered three options: American combat troops, large-scale conventional bombing, or tactical nuclear bombing. President Eisenhower consulted with Prime Minister Churchill, who expressed strong opposition to either type of air support. Eisenhower eventually decided not to send American ground soldiers because of the high likelihood of heavy casualties in the mountainous jungle terrain surrounding Dien Bien Phu. Virtually out of fresh water and medical supplies, and besieged by a force five times their own, the French troops surrendered on May 7, 1954.

In Geneva, Switzerland, the following morning, the superpowers and representatives of the two Vietnamese factions met. The Geneva Accords divided Vietnam at the seventeenth parallel, roughly corresponding to the Ben Hai River. It was further stipulated that an area extending five kilometers north and five kilometers south of this demarcation line would be a demilitarized zone (DMZ). Neither the PAVN nor the ARVN (Army of the Republic of South Vietnam) forces were allowed to establish bases or traverse this neutral boundary area, but in fact, both sides regularly violated its neutrality. Backed by the Soviet Union (U.S.S.R.) and China, Ho Chi Minh was the recognized leader of the Democratic Republic of Vietnam (DRV), commonly referred to as North Vietnam. Reluctantly supported by the United States, Bao Dai was the recognized leader of the Republic of Vietnam (RVN), commonly referred to as South Vietnam. In *A Viet Cong Memoir*, Truong Nhu Trang noted, "Vietnamese nationalism had become hostage to the ideological and geopolitical conflicts of the great powers."

There had been no thaw in the Cold War. The U.S.S.R. and Communist China were ominous forces on the international political stage, and the United States was determined to contest any spread of influence or control of what appeared to be an international communist monolith. Similarly, the U.S.S.R. was apprehensive about U.S. influence and control. Vietnam became a game board for the competing superpowers, just as Korea had been from 1950–1953, following its division and the ensuing war between American-supported South Korea and Soviet-supported North Korea.

Another key provision of the Geneva Accords was that there would be one year of free movement between North Vietnam and South Vietnam. It is estimated that nearly a million Catholics moved to the South. CIA officer Colonel Edward Lansdale headed a propaganda campaign to convince Catholics to leave the North. At the same time, about a half million Viet Minh moved back to their homes in the North, but some were encouraged by their leaders in Hanoi to remain in the South to be prepared to ensure the eventual reunification of Vietnam. A final key provision was for elections to be held in two years to reunify Vietnam.

Bao Dai was soon replaced by Ngo Dinh Diem. Born in 1901, Diem had learned to despise French rule during his years as a provincial governor and minister under Bao Dai, but when offered a position in the new government of the DRV by Ho Chi Minh,

Diem refused. He was a descendent of generations of Catholics, and hence opposed the communists. During the First Indochina War, Diem had lived in exile in the United States. There he made numerous contacts with prominent politicians in the Eisenhower administration and brandished his anticommunism and his nationalism. Diem returned to Vietnam following the Geneva Convention and, as a result of American pressure, was appointed Prime Minister by Bao Dai.

During a press conference in late 1954, President Eisenhower articulated what soon became universally referred to as the "Domino Theory." If Vietnam fell to the communists, Eisenhower asserted, soon Laos, Cambodia, and Thailand would also fall. Communism would then spread throughout Southeast Asia and continue westward into Pakistan, India, and eventually, perhaps, even the Middle East. China had already joined the communist bloc in 1950, and North Korea joined as an autonomous nation in 1953.

Senator Joe McCarthy made Eisenhower's Domino Theory seem understated. "If we lose Indochina," asserted McCarthy during a Congressional hearing (featured in de Antonio's *In the Year of the Pig*), "we will lose the Pacific and we will be an island in a communist sea." Other voices echoed McCarthy's fear, saying that if America did not fight the communists in Vietnam, America would eventually have to fight them in San Diego.

In Vietnam, the elections slated for 1956 were never held. Americans and their Vietnamese allies acknowledged that if the elections had been held then, the communists would have won by a great margin. In *An Eye for the Dragon*, historian Dennis Bloodworth commented, "This [the plan for national elections] was not among the best laid plans of mice and men, and the consequences were predictable."

One plan of the American advisors to help win support for Diem was to change his enemy's name. The Viet Minh were still respected throughout Vietnam as the patriots who defeated the French and secured Vietnamese independence. The United States Information Service (USIS) began calling them the "Viet Cong," a derogatory expression for *Viet Nam Cong San*, Vietnamese communists. Diem and his government followed suit.

From Indian Landing School to Penfield High School

My only awareness of anything even remotely connected to Vietnam was knowing that Dwight David Eisenhower was President of the United States. He was a tall, bald, smiling World War II hero. He had been a four-star general. I remember seeing him on the evening news on our black-and-white television set. He had a folksy nickname—"Ike"—and he looked like my Grandpa Wilson.

To an eight-year-old aspiring Little League star, President Eisenhower was good, brave, honest, and smart, and he wanted everyone in America to have a wonderful life. In 1956, he was running for reelection. His supporters sported "I Like Ike" buttons. I don't remember anyone not liking him, but then my politics were about as well developed as my 4' 2", 50-pound physique.

Eisenhower was reelected in 1956, and during his second term we continued to have air raid drills at the Indian Landing School. We crouched under our desks for protection from the much-anticipated Russian intercontinental ballistic missiles (ICBMs). At dinner, my parents talked about fallout shelters. I thought having another basement buried in the backyard with lots of food and water sounded neat, but I certainly didn't understand what fallout was.

I eventually made it to the majors in Little League and had the best left-handed layup on the fifth- and sixth-grade basketball team at Indian Landing. I also received a silver dollar at Indian Landing School's graduation ceremony for scoring the highest on the Iowa tests.

At about 4' 10" and 75 pounds, I headed off to Penfield Junior High School with great expectations of academic and athletic success. My world was expanding rapidly. In junior high, we had soccer practice after school every day in the fall, basketball practice in the winter, and baseball practice in the spring. After school, between seasons, my friends and I often walked the half mile to Penfield to get a soda or a float or an ice cream cone at McGowan's soda fountain.

Eisenhower was taking care of things in Washington. Mom and Dad were doing a fine job on Dale Road. And I was getting ready to go to high school—Penfield Central School in fall of 1960—at the same time that the Second Indochina War was beginning.

I didn't hear about it until my junior year at Penfield. The only wars I knew anything about were the Revolutionary War, in which we routed the redcoats to win our independence, the War of 1812 that we fought in . . . 1812, the Civil War, in which we sacked the South to win freedom for the Negroes, World War I, which we won, and World War II, which we had just won thanks to Mr. Burrell, Mr. Leonard, Mr. Mear, Mr. Jacobstein, Mr. Ellis, and my Dad.

I had yet to learn a thing about Vietnam or any country in Asia, even though I had made maps and studied every country in North America, South America, and Western Europe. I had heard a lot about Russia, but I did not understand that it was just one of fifteen republics in the Union of Soviet Socialist Republics (U.S.S.R.). Everyone just called it Russia.

As a freshman at Penfield, I took Ancient History and studied Mesopotamia, the cradle of Western Civilization—Iraq. During the fall of 1960, I remember watching some of the presidential debates between Republican Richard Nixon, Eisenhower's vice president, and Democrat Jack Kennedy. In his inaugural address, President Kennedy challenged Americans to "Ask not what your country can do for you, but what you can do for your country."

As a sophomore, I took World History and studied Western Europe. As a junior, I took American History, and in the spring I heard about Vietnam for the first time in my life.

My teacher and fellow New York Giant and Willie Mays fan, Mr. Donald Stewart, began class one day by passing out copies of *The Weekly Reader*. In it, I read about some political turmoil in a small Southeast Asian nation involving Catholics, Buddhists, and communists. All of the key figures mentioned had strange names, many beginning with "Ng . . ." No one could pronounce them, not even Mr. Stewart, and he never mentioned that Vietnamese names were written in the reverse order of American names. We read about Ngo Dinh Diem and his brother, Ngo Dinh Nhu, who were striving to build a democracy in South Vietnam, but Ho Chi Minh was not mentioned. We never studied emerging nations winning their independence from colonial powers in Africa, South America, and Asia; just the emergence of the American nation, winning its independence from Great Britain in 1776 for the benefit of all its citizens and all of their descendents.

Just as the Vietnamese names eluded our pronunciation, their political issues eluded our comprehension. That was it for high school. I don't remember ever again discussing developments in Vietnam.

Early in the afternoon on November 22, 1963, classes were interrupted by an announcement that President Kennedy had been shot. Teachers half-heartedly resumed their lessons but were soon interrupted again. President Kennedy was dead. On a cool, bright, late fall afternoon, the still-sparkling four-year-old high school filled with over a thousand energetic teenagers was absolutely silent. The typical noise and commotion of the end of the school day was absent. Everyone walked slowly and quietly to their lockers and then their buses. Some students sat on the hall floors in front of their lockers sobbing.

We went home and watched the news. We watched as Vice President Lyndon Baines Johnson of Texas was sworn in as President of the United States. We watched replays of Kennedy's motorcade rolling through Dallas until the shots struck him and Texas Governor John Connolly. Two days later, we watched the funeral. We watched a casket being pulled down Pennsylvania Avenue in Washington, D.C., as Jacqueline Kennedy and her two young children stared at it in sorrow and disbelief. That Sunday morning, I did not go to church with my parents. Instead, I stayed home and watched television as Lee Harvey Oswald was escorted out of the Dallas County Jail to be transferred to federal prison. I saw Jack Ruby break out of a crowd and fire three shots, killing Oswald.

For weeks the guilt of Oswald was argued. For months his ties to the Soviet Union were alternately established and challenged. Eventually the Warren Commission's investigation concluded that Lee Harvey Oswald, acting alone, had assassinated President Kennedy. But there were no conclusions about his motive.

Lyndon Johnson moved into the White House and continued the focus on international communism and the Soviet Union. So, too, the focus in every social studies classroom in the nation was on the Cold War. In early 1964, all seniors at Penfield were assigned research papers assessing the possibility of peaceful coexistence between the United States and the U.S.S.R. The threat of nuclear war darkened the skies all over the world from the end of World War II until the dissolution of the U.S.S.R. in the 1990s. Russia was ideologically, economically, and militarily supporting communist uprisings in undeveloped nations around the world. America was involved everywhere, too, pursuing its mission announced by President Woodrow Wilson a half-century earlier of making the world "safe for democracy." The United States and the U.S.S.R. were matching each other word for word, dollar for dollar, and M-16 for AK-47 all over the world.

I began my paper with a weak discussion of the definition of "coexistence." I had found a *New York Times* article that quoted Soviet Premier Nikita Khrushchev as stressing, "Peace is the true ally of socialism, for time is working for socialism and against capitalism."

I noted the global, European, and Asian dimensions of the conflict. "The threat of nuclear war is omnipresent. The Berlin situation waxes and wanes according to Soviet whims. Fighting continues and tension mounts in Southeast Asia." I continued, "The situation is dangerously unstable in Southeast Asia. Here the U.S. is the closest that it has been to a hot war since the Korean War. South Vietnam and Laos are the major strife torn areas. Laos is recognized as the 'plug' preventing communist infiltration into the remainder of the subcontinent. Although the U.S. has made some important gains here recently, the outcome is still far from bright."

My conclusion was optimistic about peaceful coexistence, but it one-dimensionally addressed the avoidance of nuclear war, ignoring the little problems. Like Vietnam.

The Second Indochina War Begins

While I was finishing up at Indian Landing and zooming through two years of junior high school, the Vietnamese were adjusting to freedom from the French and the demands of the Geneva Accords imposed by the superpowers.

A lot of Vietnamese were on the move. Catholics living in the Democratic Republic of Vietnam headed south, where they felt that they would be free to practice their religious beliefs. Many Viet Minh veterans living in the newly formed Republic of South Vietnam headed north, where they felt that they would be free to live according to their political and social beliefs. Although many others were confused about where to settle, most simply returned to the villages where they had been born, uninfluenced by abstract political concerns.

U.S. advisors were active in South Vietnam, striving to support a democratic anticommunist government. America's first significant action had been to pressure Bao Dai to appoint Ngo Dinh Diem as Prime Minister. In 1955, Diem organized and administered a plebiscite that ousted Bao Dai. On October 26, 1955, Diem proclaimed himself the first President of the Republic of South Vietnam.

Diem's consolidation of power was guided by Colonel Edward Lansdale, who had been active in the 1954 exodus of Catholics from the north to the south. Lansdale has been the focal point of both fiction and nonfiction about American involvement in Vietnam. He is acknowledged to be the subject of Graham Greene's novel, *The Quiet American*, and the subject of Cecil B. Currey's biography *Edward Lansdale: The Unquiet American*.

President Eisenhower immediately pledged his support to the Diem government and offered military aid, a mere three months after the U.S.S.R. had pledged its support and offered aid to Ho

Chi Minh and North Vietnam. Both governments made early errors in their attempts to solidify their power. Diem and his brother, Ngo Dinh Nhu, initiated a brutal campaign against suspected Viet Minh. Village leaders suspected of being Viet Minh were executed and replaced with leaders appointed by Diem. In the North, Ho Chi Minh's forces assailed landowners, and many were executed.

But Diem went beyond simply attacking his political adversaries. He openly favored the Catholic minority and persecuted leaders of the Buddhist majority. He also allowed large landholders to retain their property, thereby disappointing peasants who had been hoping for land reform. And, as advised by the United States, he blocked the Geneva-provided elections scheduled for 1956 on the grounds that fair elections could not be held in the North.

While renowned anticommunist and eventual National Security Council member Walter Rostow commented that Ho Chi Minh could not have been elected "dogcatcher" in the South, most other observers felt otherwise. Senator Wayne Morse, speaking in *In the Year of the Pig*, disagreed vehemently with Rostow, stating, "And you oughta have sat with me on the Foreign Relations Committee in 1956 when our intelligence forces brought in their reports warning that if the elections called for by the Geneva Accords were held, Ho Chi Minh would have been elected by at least 80 percent of the vote. And our country that boasts about believing in self-determination used its power and its prestige and its influence really to get our first puppet government under Diem not to cooperate in holding those elections. That's just a matter of historical record."

Nonetheless, during a visit to the United States in May 1957, Diem was praised by Eisenhower as the "miracle man of Asia."

Frustrated by the cancellation of the elections and other events in South Vietnam, Ho Chi Minh and his comrades abandoned pursuit of reunification simply by political means. They announced adoption of military means by declaring a "People's War" to liberate South Vietnam. Leading the struggle would be the National Front for the Liberation of South Vietnam (the

NLF)—the Viet Cong. Its formation in 1960 generally marks the beginning of the Second Indochina War, soon known as the "Vietnam War" to the Americans, and the "American War" to the Vietnamese.

To facilitate communication and the transportation of supplies from North Vietnam to the NLF, construction of what the Americans would call the "Ho Chi Minh Trail" commenced. Initially it was a virtually imperceptible 1,500-mile network of trails from the North through the dense jungle and the Truong Son Mountains on the Laos border into the South. To the North Vietnamese it was the "Truong Son Road." At first, the journey took nearly six months, but by the mid-1960s it took only three months. By 1970, it took only six weeks, and a parallel fuel pipeline had been added.

Fifteen years after the Viet Minh's first action on behalf of the peasants in Hanoi, the North Vietnamese and the NLF continued to impress observers with their ability to win the support of the common people. Quoted in PBS's *Vietnam*, American Province advisor Earl Young noted, "We continually were amazed at the professionalism—the ability to be good psychologists—that these people had. They knew exactly how to deal with the Vietnamese farmer. Now this the Americans generally never did, and the Vietnamese government might have but really wasn't that interested, so we found that a whole structure had been superimposed on this province, and it was a Viet Cong structure. They had people at every level, and they were running a shadow government coincidentally with the government's operation."

But there was a lot more going on in Vietnam than the American people were hearing about. In fact, Vietnam was still not even near the top of the list of America's political priorities. The Cold War and competition with the U.S.S.R. had held the top spot since the end of World War II, and Cuba and Laos were the specific focal points of that general international situation. After Kennedy defeated Nixon in the election of 1960, Eisenhower briefed his successor in detail about Laos and barely mentioned Vietnam.

In an April 9, 1971, column written for the *New York Times*, Billy Graham stated that following a round of golf with President Kennedy in January 1961, Kennedy had commented to Graham, "We cannot allow Laos and South Vietnam to fall to the communists." Later in 1961, the *Times* editorialized that the Vietnam War was "a struggle that this country cannot shirk."

Top Kennedy advisors General Maxwell Taylor and Walter Rostow were the first American statesmen to recommend sending combat troops to Vietnam. In October 1961, they suggested sending American soldiers disguised as flood fighters, but President Diem refused the offer, determined to keep foreign troops out of Vietnam. Ambassador Frederick Nolting, interviewed by Richard McKinzie of the Truman Library on June 30, 1975, admitted that Ho Chi Minh had been regarded by American political leaders as not primarily a nationalist, but as a communist because of his time spent in Moscow. Nolting described Diem's refusal of the offer of American troops as "prescient," sensing that their presence would only strengthen support for the Viet Cong. Echoing comments made regarding the Viet Minh leadership of the rice revolt in 1945 and Earl Young's observations about the NLF, PBS's *Vietnam* quotes American Colonel Edward Frische as saying in late 1961, "It's gonna be the man who gets the support of the farmers who's gonna eventually win this war."

In February 1962, the United States Military Assistance Command for Vietnam (MACV) was formed, replacing the Military Assistance Advisory Group dating back to 1950. In May, Vice President Lyndon Johnson visited South Vietnam and reinforced the rhetorical support of Eisenhower years earlier, calling President Diem "the Winston Churchill of Asia." Following the assassination of Kennedy, Johnson assumed the Presidency and the accompanying role as Commander in Chief of the American military forces.

In an attempt to gain control of the countryside, the strategic hamlet program was initiated. ARVN troops, supported by American advisors, forced the resettlement of thousands of rural peasants from villages controlled by the Viet Cong into fortified villages defended by local militia loyal to the Diem regime. Not only were hundreds of communities moved from their ancestral lands, but their leadership was also changed.

Brought from the Ford Motor Company to Washington as Secretary of Defense at the age of forty-four, Robert McNamara reported after visiting South Vietnam in mid-1962, "We are winning the war." But most Americans still didn't care or weren't even aware that "we" were in the war. Then a horrific scene focused the attention of the world on Vietnam.

Diem's continuing suppression of the Buddhist population exploded in Hue in May 1963, when local police and ARVN troops opened fire on Buddhists demonstrating in celebration of Buddha's birthday. One woman and eight children were killed. In June, Buddhist demonstrations continued in Saigon.

On June 11, 1963, seventy-three-year-old Buddhist monk Thich Quang Duc of Hue stepped out of a car and sat down in a lotus position in the middle of one of the main intersections in the center of Saigon. Two fellow monks doused him with gasoline. Duc lit a match and set himself on fire. David Halberstam was present. Reporting in the *New York Times*, he wrote, "As he burned he never moved a muscle, never uttered a sound, his outward composure in sharp contrast to the wailing people around him." Journalist Malcolm Browne took pictures, and they appeared on the front pages of newspapers all over the world the following morning.

After Duc's self-immolation and the ensuing international response, no film was allowed out of South Vietnam until it had been developed and checked by South Vietnamese officials. President Diem's sister-in-law, Madame Ngo Dinh Nhu, is shown in PBS's *Vietnam* flippantly commenting, "Oh, they have barbecued one of their monks."

Diem's nepotistic regime had been exposed as arrogant, corrupt, and repressive. Eisenhower's "miracle man" and Johnson's "Winston Churchill" was described by President Kennedy as "out of touch with his people." Some generals talked about ousting him, but they were apprehensive about losing American support. Following six months of complicated discussions between rebel generals and Kennedy administration representatives, during which both sides vacillated, CIA officer Lucien Conein told the

Thich Quang Duc, a Buddhist monk, burns himself to death on a Saigon street on June 11, 1963, to protest alleged persecution of Buddhists by the South Vietnamese government. © AP/Wide World Photos.

conspirators that the United States would not interfere with their planned coup.

Propped up by American economic and military support, Diem was still an individual who spoke for himself. PBS's *Vietnam* shows him explaining, "I am an anti-communist from the point of view of doctrine, but I am not an anti-communist from the point of view of politics and humanity. I consider the communists as brothers. We are a little country and we only want to live in peace."

On November 1, 1963, ARVN soldiers surrounded the Presidential Palace and seized police headquarters. Diem and his brother Nhu escaped to Cholon, the Chinese sector of Saigon. A few hours later they surrendered but were assassinated the morning of November 2. Throughout the following days, years, and decades, some believed that Diem was assassinated because he was secretly negotiating with Ho Chi Minh and North Vietnam.

Three weeks after Diem's assassination, President Kennedy was assassinated in Dallas. Stepping into the presidency, Johnson announced that he would not "lose Vietnam," and by the end of 1963 there were over 16,000 American advisors in Vietnam. Supposedly not involved in combat, these advisors were primarily pilots, helicopter crewmen, Marines, and Army infantrymen training the ARVN.

In July 1964, the Republicans nominated Barry Goldwater to run against Johnson. I remember Goldwater. He was a "hawk." He was an intensely anticommunist conservative who wanted to increase America's military role in Vietnam. Although my awareness of Vietnam and the issues being played out there were just developing, I would have voted against Goldwater. But in 1964, the voting age was still twenty-one. Not until the passage of the 26th Amendment in 1971 were eighteen year olds granted the right to vote. So, this eighteen year old spent another apolitical summer working for his Dad changing tires and making deliveries, playing basketball every evening at Penfield, and getting ready to go to college in the fall.

Trinity College

During the fall of my senior year at Penfield, I visited Trinity College in Hartford, Connecticut, and Wesleyan University in Middletown, Connecticut. Wesleyan's representative was quite impressed with his school's academic reputation and its athletic prowess. Trinity's representative was quite impressed with my grades and SAT scores and acknowledged that most of Trinity's athletes had not been high school All Stars. He encouraged me to apply for early admission. I did and was accepted before Christmas.

Through my high school and college years, the draft and American involvement in Vietnam were on the distant periphery of my life. As a college student, I was deferred from draft eligibility. I had read and heard a little about American military advisors and the Viet Cong and the Domino Theory, but I was primarily interested in basketball and cars and girls.

They were at the center of my life. Despite having been only a sub at Penfield, I made the varsity at Trinity. I bought my first car, a black, four-door 1958 Chevrolet Impala, in the summer of 1966 between my sophomore and junior years. And I had a girlfriend who attended Saint Joseph's College in nearby West Hartford.

Peers were burning their draft cards, but that reality and the imminence of the draft were not factors in my daily life. My friends and I had many "What if I got drafted?" discussions, but the possibility of being in the military still seemed so remote for us that our conversations were more like creative thinking exercises than actual consideration of plans for the future.

As a college student, I was quite intensely, unconsciously apolitical. When I picked up a newspaper, I turned to the sports pages. When I was home for vacations or in the summers, I seldom joined my parents in their evening ritual of watching the news before dinner, and I rarely looked at the weekly issues of *Time* that arrived in our mailbox every Tuesday. But during my junior year at Trinity, while sitting in the waiting room of my dentist's office, an issue of *Esquire* caught my eye. On its black cover, a quotation in bold, white letters grabbed my attention.

For a half dozen years, the United States had been involved in Vietnam. I had paid little attention to either the government's pronouncements about the need to stop the spread of communism, or its opponents' proclamations against interfering in the domestic affairs of independent nations. But I picked up that magazine and read John Sack's entire "account of one company of American soldiers in Fort Dix, New Jersey, who trained for war and found it fifty days later in Vietnam." The article had a lasting impact on my developing perspective on Vietnam and my perspective on my own country.

Following eight weeks of basic training and a brief leave, M company flew to Saigon, prepared for war by "two months of training and years of John Wayne," wrote Sack. One new arrival asked, "Any action around here?" Sack wrote, "M Company was to have an answer soon enough."

From Saigon the company flew by helicopter to the Central Highlands and learned that they were joining Vietnam's jinxed battalion. Its fate was to encounter Viet Cong everywhere it went, and it had the highest casualty rate of any American unit. Sack's soldiers were to be choppered "into Charlie's heartland"—to be dropped off behind enemy lines just south of a former Michelin plantation. Their mission, as delivered by Lieutenant Colonel Smoke, was to "Kill VC!" I could not put the magazine down.

On their treks through the jungle and over paths through rice fields and into villages, they burned homes and shot themselves accidentally. Twice they were ambushed. A Vietnamese soldier traveling with M company was responsible for sanctioning "any or all burning or blowing up, first having satisfied himself that the rice in each cache was truly communist, this soldier having been trained in this mystic art," wrote Sack.

Outside one small village, one soldier reported having been

shot at. M company stormed ahead. Sack described the attack: "Taking their wild revenge, the irrepressible privates went though the yellow Vietnamese village like Visigoths, like Sherman's army, burning the huts, ripping the clothes, breaking the jars, the rice running out onto the muddy floors . . . until there was nothing left."

The Lieutenant Colonel's directive had been qualified by his insistence that his troops "insure that positive identification is made." They were to kill only VC. But that day, their platoon leader, Sergeant Gore, told them to "Kill everything. Destroy everything. Kill the cows, the pigs, the chickens, everything."

"Then it was that the incident happened," wrote Sack. A grenade was tossed into a hole in the floor of a hut. Peering in to assess the damage, a soldier shouted, 'Oh my God—we hit a little girl.' The child's nose was bleeding and there was a hole in the back of her skull." Sack quoted a lieutenant commenting later about the incident as saying, "These people don't want us here anyhow. Why should I care about them?"

Sack's chronicle made me care about the Vietnamese people and about the parents and the children of the American soldiers who were being sent to fight in an environment they could not navigate against enemies they could not identify for a cause they did not understand. Reading the article crystallized my previously vague sense of what was happening in Vietnam, and simultaneously contradicted all of the values that I had learned growing up as a Christian and as an American.

Then I went to the gym and put on my sneakers for basketball practice, and worried about beating Wesleyan. I forgot about all of the Vietnamese and Americans who were dying on the other side of the world.

One of my fraternity brothers—Anthony "Buddy" Kupka— wanted to enlist in the Marines and go to Vietnam and fight. No one could understand him. Most of us were so immersed in our own cultural experience that we didn't want to go anywhere else in the world, except maybe Western Europe, even just to visit, let alone to live . . . or to die. Buddy enlisted in the Marines and completed basic training and Officer Candidate School in the summer of 1967 between our junior and senior years. He figured that it would save him some time after graduation and help him get in shape for his senior football season, too.

I also learned that summer that a close friend from my neighborhood was in the Marines. Jim Rattigan was a year older than me, a kid who I had always looked up to because he was a good athlete. He was a star on Penfield's championship soccer team, and a starting guard on its basketball team. At about 5' 8", "Rat" was always about a half foot taller and much stronger than I was. Until the summer between my sophomore and junior years, when I grew seven inches to 5' 11".

Rat graduated from Nichols College in Massachusetts in 1967 and joined the Marines. After officer training and being commissioned a Second Lieutenant, Rat was sent to Vietnam. He spent the majority of his two one-year tours in combat in the Central Highlands, where the defoliant Agent Orange was used extensively.

Even the first reports from Vietnam during the Tet Offensive had little impact on my friends and me, even though we had just started the second semester of our senior year and knew that we would soon be out of college. But on February 2, 1968, right before dinner, our attention was caught by a film clip from Saigon. Piled up on the battered couches and chairs in our fraternity's TV room, we saw a Vietnamese police officer shoot a plaid-shirted Vietnamese civilian in the head. Walter Cronkite explained that the man was suspected of being a Viet Cong.

"Did you see that?" asked my friend Bob Gutzman. Obviously we had, but while some of us expressed our astonishment loudly, others were so stunned by seeing a real killing that they were speechless. None of our history lessons, none of the books we read as kids, none of Hollywood's finest movies had prepared us for the harsh black-and-white reality of blood spurting out of the side of a man's head as he collapsed lifelessly.

But the next day we were foolish frat boys again, primarily concerned about winning the intramural softball championship, and planning how to balance our plans for a graduation celebration with our parents' desires to see the friends that they had

South Vietnamese National Police Chief Brig Gen. Nguyen Ngoc Loan executes a suspected Viet Cong officer with a single pistol shot in the head in Siagon, Vietnam, on February 1, 1968. © AP/Wide World Photos.

made on Parents' Weekends and with getting our clothes, books, and stereos packed up for the trip home.

That May weekend arrived faster than any of us had expected. When Trinity's Class of 1968 graduated, Buddy Kupka received a diploma and a commission as a Second Lieutenant in the U.S. Marines. The seventeen of us cut loose from our parents after dinner and got together around the jukebox in the basement of Sigma Nu for one last night of too much beer and too little sleep. Some guys made it upstairs to their beds, but others just collapsed on the couches in the living room. Some even settled for the floor. One by one awakenings and "Good-byes" broke up the Sunday morning. Jim Stuhlman drove 500 miles back to Ohio with his Mom and Dad. Bob Gutzman flew 2,000 miles back to Idaho with his parents. Bob Heimgartner just drove four miles out to his family's home in Wethersfield, a Hartford suburb.

Buddy Kupka got married right after graduation, and then reported for active duty. He received his orders for Vietnam early in 1969, but his wife was pregnant, and he was given the option of postponing his departure until after the birth of his child. While visiting some of his Trinity classmates, he said that he knew he wasn't coming back. They urged him to stay home until his child was born. He told them, "I just want to get it over with."

On April 16, 1969, Marine Second Lieutenant Anthony Edward Kupka was killed by multiple fragmentation wounds in combat in Quang Nam. He was buried in Arlington Cemetery in May of 1969. He had been killed by a grenade near Da Nang almost exactly a year after his graduation and marriage, just three days after the birth of his daughter and a month before I reported for basic training at Lackland Air Force Base in San Antonio, Texas.

American Escalation

In the summer of 1964, while I had been preparing to go off to Trinity, perhaps the single most critical incident in the history of American involvement in Vietnam occurred.

Operation Plan 34A was a CIA covert operation that sent ARVN commandoes in American-supplied speedboats to strike radar sites along the coastline of North Vietnam. The destroyer USS *Maddox* was patrolling the Gulf of Tonkin using electronic surveillance to locate the radar sites and supporting the ARVN raids.

On August 2, 1964, three North Vietnamese patrol boats fired on the *Maddox*, but inflicted no casualties. U.S. Navy fighters from the aircraft carrier *Ticonderoga* retaliated, sinking one patrol boat and damaging the other two.

On August 3, the *Maddox* and the *C. Turner Joy*, another destroyer, moved within eight miles of the coast. Darkness and thunderstorms confused crewmembers, who could not determine if they were under attack again.

Despite knowing that there were reasons for the first day's North Vietnamese attack and being unsure of what had actually happened the following day, President Johnson addressed Congress. He decried "deliberate unprovoked attacks" on U.S. ships and their crews, and he requested authorization to use force as deemed necessary to defend U.S. troops. Senator William Fullbright hurried the Gulf of Tonkin Resolution through Congress in just two days. The House of Representatives voted unanimously for it, and the Senate voted 88–2 in favor of it. Only Senators Wayne Morse of Oregon and Ernest Gruening of Alaska opposed the resolution. Morse appears in PBS's *Vietnam* saying, "History is going to record that Senator Gruening and I voted in the interest of the American people this morning against this resolution. I'd have the American people remember what the resolution really is. It's a resolution which seeks to give the President of the United States the power to make war without a declaration of war."

What happened in the Gulf of Tonkin has been referred to as a minor incident with major consequences. That may be an understatement. Even Alexander Haig acknowledges the misrepresentation of the incident. Former Navy pilot, POW, and Ross Perot's vice presidential running mate James Stockdale was flying above the Gulf of Tonkin on August 3. He stated in CNN's *Cold War: Vietnam* documentary, "There was nothing there but black water and American firepower." Many feel that Johnson had the resolution prepared even before the incident, and he later commented, "For all I know our Navy was shooting at whales out there."

In November 1964, President Johnson was elected with 61 percent of the popular vote, the biggest winning margin in history at the time. In December, a fourth coup in South Vietnam in less than a year replaced older ARVN officers with a cadre of younger ones led by Nguyen Van Thieu and Nguyen Cao Ky. By year's end there were over 23,000 American advisors in Vietnam.

Although Johnson's top priority was his Great Society domestic program, he was soon drawn inextricably into what historian David Halberstam labeled the Vietnam "quagmire." In March 1965, American combat troops joined the advisors. Two battalions—3,500 Marines—were sent to Da Nang to defend the American air base there. Within a month, they were authorized to conduct offensive operations. Also in March, Johnson authorized Operation Rolling Thunder, the bombing of North Vietnam. Although originally planned to last just eight weeks, Rolling Thunder continued for three years.

Even in the midst of such dramatic decisions, Johnson had a sense of their futility. He acknowledged his anxiety (on tape) to McNamara, saying, "I don't see anything is going to be as bad as losing, and I don't see any way of winning."

Undersecretary of State George Ball has said in PBS's *Vietnam* that at the time, "I was convinced that we would never break the will of a determined people simply by bombing and in fact we would probably tend to unite them even more than ever."

Later, as reported by PBS, Pham Van Dong confirmed the accuracy of Ball's prediction. "It must not be forgotten that [U.S. Air Force Commander in Chief] General Curtis LeMay has said that the U.S. should bomb Vietnam back into the Stone Age," noted Dong, "but they were greatly mistaken. Bombing only caused the people to be more resilient and more resolute."

By the end of 1967, nearly every military target in North Vietnam had been damaged or destroyed, but the war was far from over. Despite the frequent bombing of the main bridge over the Red River in Hanoi, military, commercial, and civilian traffic still flowed. After the American bombing destroyed the steel and concrete bridge, the North Vietnamese constructed a pontoon bridge in sections that they assembled after dark each evening and dissembled before dawn each morning.

In the spring of 1965, however, virtually every American involved in Vietnam policy decisions feared that South Vietnam and its army were on the verge of collapse. When nearly a hundred top military officers and civilian politicians gathered in Saigon following another governmental crisis, the group was asked, "Anyone want to be Prime Minister?" Following a brief silence, Nguyen Van Thieu said, "I propose Ky." Ky later explained that his only talent was as a pilot and military leader, and he deferred to his nominator. Within a month, Thieu and Ky assumed power as President and Prime Minister respectively. Their government was the tenth in twenty months in South Vietnam.

In the United States, the draft was increased. More and more young men were summoned to serve. And more and more young men refused to serve. Some burned their draft cards publicly. Some fled to Canada privately.

Antiwar demonstrations increased, and triggered counter-demonstrations in support of the war. On April 17, 1965, 15,000 Americans in Washington, D.C., protested the bombing of North Vietnam. On October 30, 25,000 Americans in New York City marched in support of the war. By the end of the year, there were 185,000 American soldiers in Vietnam, but the Viet Cong still controlled about half of the countryside.

That same year, the Department of Defense produced a film

entitled *Why Vietnam*. It was provided to the public as a "service of your government," but today it bears the disclaimer, "This program has been declared obsolete within the sponsoring agency, but may have value for educational use." The narrator of the film repeatedly mispronounces the name of the country, referring to it as "vee-et-nam" (as in "am") instead of "vyet-nom" (as in "nominate"). He introduces the film by mentioning Hitler and Mussolini, and then stresses America's commitment "to help a free people protect their sovereignty." According to the narrator, the South Vietnamese are being threatened by "Ho Chi Minh, the communist leader of North Vietnam ... (He) plays the kindly, smiling grandfather, but behind the smile is a mind which is planning a reign of terror in South Vietnam." The film concludes by reiterating America's proud stand against a global communist plan. "Once again, half a world away has become our front door. If freedom is to survive in any American hometown, it must be preserved in places such as South Vietnam."

In early 1966, large-scale search and destroy operations were conducted in an attempt to gain control of the countryside in South Vietnam. Searching and destroying typically featured rounding up elders, women, and children and leading them away from villages that were then burned to the ground because their residents were suspected of supporting the Viet Cong.

General William Westmoreland was Commander in Chief of MACV. His goal was to engage and defeat the enemy wherever they could be found. Military leaders placed increasing significance on "body counts" as a means of demonstrating the progress and success of the American war effort. Marine Lieutenant Phillip Caputo was one of the first American combat soldiers to arrive in Da Nang. He recalls the Marines' attitude as being similar to that of their political and military leaders, perhaps to that of all Americans. "Being U.S. Marines, we thought our mere presence in Vietnam was going to terrify the enemy into quitting." This attitude was carried off the air base at Da Nang, through the rice paddies, and into the jungles and over the mountainous trails accompanied by the unofficial body-counting principle: "If it's dead and it's Vietnamese, it's Viet Cong." A decade later, Caputo returned to

Vietnam to cover the evacuation of Saigon for the *Chicago Tribune*, and he subsequently authored *A Rumor of War*.

This unwritten post-combat accounting principle simultaneously inflated reports of American combat successes and concealed civilian casualties, establishing a mind-set that may have contributed to atrocities such as those that occurred at My Lai in the spring of 1968. During 1966, the American troop presence in Vietnam more than doubled to approximately 390,000.

Also in 1966, Senator Fullbright dramatically articulated his change in perspective. The Congressman who had led the swift passage of the Gulf of Tonkin Resolution just two years earlier published *The Arrogance of Power*, detailing the misdeeds of the Johnson administration.

At the same time that the antiwar protests were increasing in both frequency and scale, former Vice President Nixon asserted that they were "prolonging the war." Many others felt that Americans who publicly expressed their opposition to the war were aiding the enemy—North Vietnam and the Viet Cong. General Westmoreland echoed Nixon's perspective with a significant qualification. He felt that the protestors were giving the Vietnamese communists hope that they could politically win the war that they were losing militarily.

Every clash between American soldiers and either the North Vietnamese regulars or the Viet Cong was "won" by the Americans. Official accounts always reported many more enemy soldiers killed and wounded than Americans.

During the first major U.S. ground operation at Chu Lai, forty-five Marines were reported killed and 120 wounded while killing 614 Viet Cong. In November, during the battle in the Ia Drang Valley depicted in the movie *We Were Soldiers*, seventy-nine Army infantrymen were reported killed and 121 wounded while killing and wounding an estimated 2,000 North Vietnamese soldiers. Despite the disparity in casualties, both sides claimed victory. "This was our first defeat of the Americans," claimed General Giap. Westmoreland was incredulous at Giap's attitude, commenting later, "The attitude of the enemy was not comparable . . . he was ready, willing and able to pay a far greater price then we Caucasians would."

In the early months of 1966, during large-scale search and destroy missions against both Viet Cong and NVA regulars, 228 Americans were killed and 788 wounded while killing 1,342 of the enemy. At Ap Gu, the largest military offensive of the war at that time, 282 Americans were killed compared to 2,728 Viet Cong. In May 1967, at Khe Sanh, only 155 Americans were killed compared to 940 North Vietnamese soldiers. All these numerical victories led Johnson to announce proudly, "We are inflicting greater losses than we are taking. . . . We are making progress."

But the country was divided in its response to the optimism of its leaders. Some Americans believed that it was essential to stop the spread of communism, and Vietnam was the right place to do it. Others believed that Vietnam's problems were internal political problems and should not be cause for American interference. And the boys and men who were sent over to fight were learning how complicated the situation was. Their preparation had trained them to fight a conventional war against the Soviets in Europe. They had not been prepared for either guerilla warfare or tropical jungles. One GI speaking in PBS's *Vietnam* explained, "It's not like the San Francisco 49ers on one side of the field and the Cincinnati Bengals on the other. You never knew who was an enemy and who was a friend. They were all Vietnamese. They all looked alike."

Belatedly, Westmoreland concurred. Speaking of Vietnam in CNN's *Cold War* series, the retired general who had led men in combat in World War II, Korea, and Vietnam acknowledged, "This [Vietnam] was a type of war that we had no experience with before."

Another GI recalled his school lessons when analyzing his experience in Vietnam. "In grade school," he explained, "we learned about Redcoats—the nasty British soldiers who tried to stifle our freedom and the tyranny of George III. I think again subconsciously but not very subconsciously, I began to increasingly have the feeling that I was a Redcoat, and I think it was one of the most staggering realizations of my life to suddenly understand I wasn't a hero. I wasn't a good guy. I wasn't handing out candy and cigarettes to the kids in the French villages . . . that somehow I had become everything that I had learned to believe was evil."

Westmoreland, however, was confident. He had been named *Time*'s Man of the Year in 1965, and had been widely quoted as saying, "I hope they try something because we are looking for a fight." Others in President Johnson's inner sanctum did not share the commander's enthusiasm. McGeorge Bundy (National Security Advisor under Presidents Kennedy and Johnson), George Ball (Undersecretary of State), and Bill Moyers (Special Assistant to Johnson) all resigned their positions due to disagreements with the policies of escalating American involvement.

President Johnson was doubly troubled. Not only was the war in Vietnam a growing problem, but it was also diminishing the administrative and financial resources that could be allocated to supporting his Great Society domestic vision. In late 1967, Reverend Dr. Martin Luther King proclaimed, "The promises of the Great Society have been shot down on the battlefield of Vietnam."

More shots were imminent. Despite the arrival of nearly a half million American soldiers in Vietnam in two and a half years, the North Vietnamese and Viet Cong had not been significantly weakened. In the first days of 1968, they were planning and coordinating a massive strike throughout South Vietnam to coincide with the celebration of Tet, the Vietnamese New Year.

On January 21, 1968, the NVA struck the American base at Khe Sanh. Ten days later, the full-scale Tet Offensive was launched with attacks on virtually every major city and provincial capital in South Vietnam. Often described as the turning point of the war, the 1968 Tet Offensive did not achieve its goals. North Vietnamese planners anticipated a strong South Vietnamese civilian uprising in support of their military actions, but it did not occur. U.S. forces regrouped strongly from the initial strikes, and repelled the Viet Cong and NVA attackers everywhere. In Ben Tre, south of Saigon, Army troops repelled a VC attack using total force. An unnamed Army officer was widely quoted as saying, "We had to destroy it [Ben Tre] in order to save it." But other sources assert that the quote was fabricated because it made good copy. A single sentence whose origin is hotly debated forty years later. Just like thousands of other details about the war, not to mention the war itself.

Later that year, commenting on the effects in North Vietnam of the intensive bombing of Rolling Thunder, Ho Chi Minh said, "The village is not destroyed even when it is destroyed." Another of Ho's expressions of his dedication to attaining his goal.

Americans from Los Angeles to Boston and from Milwaukee to Dallas saw the Tet Offensive and the American retaliation on their televisions every evening. They saw the dead bodies of the Viet Cong commandoes who had broken into the U.S. Embassy compound in Saigon the day before. They saw American boys dying in the mud in Khe Sanh. And they heard one soldier comment, while firing his M-16 over a wall in Hue, "This whole thing stinks really."

A month later, they saw South Vietnamese General Nguyen Ngoc Loan shoot a suspected Viet Cong guerilla in the right side of his head. Eddie Adams' photo of the execution was on the front page of newspapers across the United States and around the world. It earned Adams a Pulitzer Prize. Film of the execution, including the blood spurting out of the left side of the suspected Viet Cong's head, was shown on the NBC evening news that evening. That's the clip that caught the attention of me and my fraternity brothers in our senior year at Trinity.

That image of the apparently vicious Loan executing an apparently defenseless and unidentifiable man is one of the myriad ironies of the war. Adams later wished that he had never taken it. Assigned by his Associated Press bureau chief to follow Loan after the incident, Adams learned that General Loan was a hero to both his troops and civilians in South Vietnam. Minutes before the photo, several of Loan's men had been killed by this man. One victim had been at home with his wife and children.

"I killed the general with my camera," wrote Adams in *Time* magazine. "Still photographs are the most powerful weapons in the world. People believe them, but photographs do lie, even without manipulation. They are only half-truths. What the photograph didn't say was 'What would you have done if you were the general at that time and place on that hot day, and you caught the so-called bad guy after he blew away one, two, or three American soldiers?' "

About a month after Tet, CBS anchorman Walter Cronkite, probably the most trusted newsman in America, returned from a trip to Saigon and predicted during the CBS evening news that "The bloody experience of Vietnam is to end in a stalemate." At the same time, and for the second time in six months, General Westmoreland was requesting over 200,000 additional combat troops for Vietnam. In response to his initial request in the summer of 1967, President Johnson had agreed to only 45,000.

Secretary of Defense McNamara finally walked out of the Pentagon at the end of February 1968. For months, if not years, he had opposed many of the military and political increases in support for South Vietnam. Following Tet and confronted by further requests to bolster the American military presence, McNamara resigned his post, and moved to New York to lead the World Bank. In March, Clark Clifford replaced McNamara. He immediately conducted a comprehensive study of America involvement in Vietnam that concluded that military victory was not likely.

While American soldiers were fighting battles in Vietnam, President Johnson was fighting for ballots in America. He narrowly defeated antiwar Democrat challenger Eugene McCarthy in the New Hampshire presidential primary, and just days later, Robert Kennedy announced his candidacy for the Democratic nomination.

Bombarded by criticism from outside and inside his party, and frustrated by the war's interference with his domestic programs, Johnson pondered his future as he prepared to address the nation in late March. His speechwriters were revising the draft late into the evening of March 30, 1968. The next morning, Johnson was told that it was all set except for a conclusion. "I may have a little ending of my own," replied Johnson obliquely. That evening, he concluded his address to the nation by stating, "I shall not seek and I will not accept the nomination of my party for another term as your President."

I watched Johnson's announcement in the kitchen of my apartment in Hartford. I was a senior at Trinity with only an intramural softball season and four final exams between me and graduation. I was aware of America's involvement in Vietnam, but disinterested. Our TV sat atop our refrigerator, usually turned on, but seldom noted. Johnson caught my attention that evening. A tall, heavyset, imposing man, leader of the most powerful nation in the world, Johnson projected only powerlessness.

Less than a week later, Dr. Martin Luther King Jr. was assassinated in Memphis, Tennessee, triggering civil and racial uprisings in over one hundred American cities. Paralleling the civil disturbances were continuing antiwar demonstrations. In Vietnam, three months after the initial NVA strike at Khe Sanh, MACV shut down its air base there and withdrew the Marines. Johnson summed up the siege at Khe Sanh as having proven the futility of enemy attempts to win a military victory. An NVA officer called the closing of the base America's worst defeat.

In California, Robert Kennedy was assassinated immediately after his triumph in that state's presidential primary. Moderate Hubert Humphrey won the Democratic nomination, but he was narrowly defeated by Republican Richard Nixon, who had promised "an honorable end to the war in Vietnam." Nixon brought Harvard professor Henry Kissinger to Washington as his National Security Advisor.

A Year of Uncertainty: From Trinity to Basic Training

I graduated from Trinity in May of 1968 lacking direction. I had once planned on going to law school because I knew that it was an easy route to wealth. I had taken the law boards during the spring of my senior year but had not applied to any law schools for two reasons: My draft status was uncertain, and I was tired of going to school.

As more and more young American males were being drafted and sent to Vietnam and the numbers of killed and injured mounted, more and more attention was being paid to who was being drafted and who was not. There were disproportionate numbers of young nonwhite and working class men being drafted, being sent to Vietnam, and eventually going into combat. Middle- and upper-class white males were avoiding the draft through college and other deferments, avoiding service in Vietnam when drafted, and avoiding combat when serving in Vietnam.

To determine more fairly who would serve in the military, two significant changes to the draft were approved by Congress for implementation in December 1969. Graduate school deferments were to be abolished, and a lottery was designed to determine who was drafted on the basis of birth dates rather than race, ethnicity, or family socioeconomic status. I figured that I'd just tread water until I found out whether I was going to be drafted or not.

Even if my birth date, June 30 was not a date selected in the lottery, I still didn't want to keep going to school. I had had enough for a while. I painted houses the summer after graduation, and I began to think seriously about my beliefs and my future. I realized that my years of just doing homework and playing basketball were over. I also kept thinking about the article about M Company that I had read in *Esquire*.

In those months of limbo, I often discussed the American involvement in Vietnam with my father. One such discussion was particularly heated.

Dad had grown up in South Byron, a small town in upstate New York about twenty miles west of Rochester. He was born in 1913, the third of five boys. He had gone to a one-room school, and his first trip to the big city of Rochester was over dirt roads. One summer during the Depression, his parents loaned him to a farmer just so there would be one less boy to feed at the Coward dinner table.

Because his older brother Todd had had problems as a sixteen-year-old at the University of Rochester, Dad was sent to the Lancaster Preparatory School in Buffalo before heading further west to continue his education at the University of Michigan.

After graduating from Michigan, he worked for Proctor and Gamble in Buffalo. After Pearl Harbor was attacked, he enlisted in the Army.

He asked his sweetheart Anna Grace Wilson to marry him. After basic training he would have a two-week leave, and he wanted to arrange the wedding then. Anna Grace loved him, but she didn't want to have a husband for a couple days and then say "Good-bye," not knowing if she would ever see him again. Dad was sent to the Aleutian Islands to protect Alaska from the Japanese. He sent Mom a dozen red roses every month for a year.

They were married on June 3, 1944, after his tour in the Aleutians was completed. Dad served until the end of the war, and I was born in 1946. In the summer of 1951, we moved into a new house on Dale Road, which would be the family home for forty years.

At twenty-two, however, I was paying attention to the world beyond the boundaries of my childhood. My political apathy was disappearing. I did not want to go to Vietnam, not because I was afraid, but because I believed that what was going on over there was wrong. I tried to explain that to Dad.

We sat across from each other at the kitchen table. This was not one of our beer-and-popcorn chats about an upcoming Michigan–Ohio State football game. Or even a pre-election Nixon–Humphrey debate. This was a strong-coffee, elbows-on-the-table, father-versus-son argument about a war.

He kept repeating, "I served in World War II. I don't understand why you won't now."

"Dad, this is different," I countered. "Hitler was trying to kill all the Jews in Europe, and his armies already occupied France, and were looking at England, and the Japanese had destroyed Pearl Harbor. Vietnam is no threat to the U.S."

"It's communism. And Russia wants to take over the world. We've got to stop them somewhere," he insisted.

"They're not in Vietnam, Dad," I noted.

"Look, Russ, I don't want you to have to go to a war, but if anyone's son has to go, then everyone's son has to go."

"No one's son should go, Dad. Most of the guys fighting and dying over there are kids younger than me. They couldn't survive in the jungle by themselves even if there wasn't a war."

"Who do you think fought the Germans?" asked Dad, "Not thirty-year-old veterans. Thousands of teenagers who barely knew how to shoot an M-1."

"At least they could tell who the enemy was," I fired back. "In Vietnam, you can't tell a civilian from a soldier. You can't tell a South Vietnamese from a North Vietnamese. And I don't even half understand who the Viet Cong are."

"The South Vietnamese wear uniforms," said Dad, "and they're fighting with our troops. And the North Vietnamese have uniforms, too. Or weapons. Civilians wouldn't be carrying rifles."

"Dad, I read an article in *Esquire* about how our troops are doing more bad than good over there. They're killing old men and women and children."

"I watch the news every night," he said, "and I hear that we're helping South Vietnam set up a democratic government and training their soldiers so that they can take over the fighting."

"Oh, Dad. You just don't understand," I sighed. "America has more right to go into Czechoslovakia than into Vietnam. You know the Russians just rolled their tanks into Prague and shut it down, right?"

"Of course I know that," he said, "but we can't risk nuclear war."

"I'd rather go to Czechoslovakia and fight and maybe die myself," I asserted, "than have any more guys die in Vietnam," I said.

"Oh, you don't even know if you'll get drafted," he replied. "You don't even know if you'll go to Vietnam. Not everyone goes."

"That's not the point, Dad."

That fall I received a letter from the Selective Service. My destiny was not going to be determined by the first draft lottery after all. I had an "Order to Report for Armed Services Physical Examination" at the Federal Building in Buffalo. At the time, I had not considered going to Canada, and I certainly was not thinking about going to prison, so I figured I had three options.

Philosophically, I initiated an application for Conscientious Objector (CO) status. I did conscientiously object to war. Quite simply, I did not think people should be killing each other. And I did not feel that Vietnam's political conflict threatened the freedom of Americans to see the USA in their Chevrolets, as Dinah Shore sang every Sunday evening at 8:00.

Pragmatically, I gathered letters from my doctors attesting to my physical ailments—asthma and a hiatal hernia—hoping that they would earn me IV-F (Registrant not qualified for military service) status.

And finally, in what I would later call an "existential compromise," I investigated noncombat service options. I contacted the Air Force recruiter and was scheduled to take the Air Force Officer Qualifying Test (AFOQT).

When I boarded the bus for Buffalo, I had taken care of all three. I had submitted a CO application, was carrying letters from two doctors, and had taken the AFOQT. One letter documented my allergies. Hay fever and asthma had affected me all of my life. Some days every August, I sneezed so often that I barely had time to breathe. Some days every October, I wheezed so badly that I almost suffocated. The other letter described a hiatal hernia, discovered during my senior year at Trinity. I really believed that my medical history would be my "Get Out of Jail Free" pass.

Although I had played basketball for three hours the day before the trip to Buffalo, the letters I carried described a young man more suited for an ICU than a firefight. Over fifty of us were herded into a stale room in an old World War I armory in Buffalo. An old sergeant grunted, "Does anyone have a letter from a doctor?" Almost everyone raised a hand.

He changed his question. "Does anyone *not* have a letter from a doctor?" Three hands were raised. Those guys went off, and the rest of us lined up for assessments of our allegedly incapacitating disabilities.

We did deep knee bends.

Our feet and arches were checked.

We went into padded telephone booths for hearing tests.

Our vision and color vision were checked.

About a dozen of us who had passed these tests were lined up waiting for a doctor to check our lungs. Standing shoulder to shoulder, we could just as easily have been toeing the starting line for a five-mile race. A short, hunched over major ambled toward us, stethoscope dangling from his neck.

After passing four guys and dismissing one, he faced me and read the letter attesting to my asthmatic history. I smelled smoke on his uniform and saw a pack of Marlboros in his front shirt pocket. He wheezed something about my looking pretty healthy and placed his stethoscope on the left side of my chest. He asked me to breathe deeply. He repeated this on the right side. "Sounds pretty good to me," he wheezed. I had passed.

I was classified 1-A, "Available for military service," and told that my induction notice would come soon in the mail. I got back on the bus for Rochester, gazed out the window through the darkness and rain. I knew that I could never kill anyone. I thought about Canada or prison.

Just as the war was escalating, so, too, was my sense that it was wrong. So many purported experts were saying so many different things about the culture and politics of Vietnam. It was clear that there were no American experts on Vietnam.

After my physical, I had only two options left. I soon learned that my CO application had been rejected because I did not have a supporting letter from a reverend or a minister. Then I received a call from my Air Force recruiter saying that my test results were in, and I should come down and discuss them.

I had crashed the section on piloting, but my eyesight disqualified me for pilot or navigator duty. My total score, however, still qualified me for Officer Candidate School (OCS), and on February 5, 1969, I enlisted under the Delayed Enlistment Program, assured that by the time I reported for Basic Training, there would be a slot for me in OCS.

I was told that I had at least three months before I would have to report for duty. I packed up my clothes and sneaks and golf clubs and skis, and headed west. I drove to Pullman, Washington, where my friends Bob and Melva Gutzman were living. Bob had been attending law school just across the border at the University of Idaho and Melva was teaching second grade in Pullman. When I got there, Bob had dropped out of law school.

He was not worried about the draft because he had blown out his right knee in the opening basketball game of our senior year at Trinity. It wouldn't bend enough for Bob to be a soldier. He was IV-F. He was so disabled that he beat me in every one-on-one basketball game we played during my stay in Pullman. We both got jobs working for Puregro, a large northwestern fertilizer company. It was springtime in the Northwest, and the farmers were planting and fertilizing. We were hired to deliver supplies to farms throughout eastern Washington and western Idaho.

One March morning, we were told to sweep the warehouse. I started at one end, and Bob started at the other. I paused and looked across the warehouse floor. There was my friend Bob wielding his broom like a pro. We had sat in calculus, history, and English classes together. We had played football, basketball, and baseball together. He had a BA in History and I had a BA in English, and we were sweeping a warehouse floor for two dollars an hour.

In early May, I got a call from my parents saying that the letter from the Air Force had come and that I had to report to Lackland on the nineteenth. I finished the week at work, paid a fourteen-year-old kid to tune up my 1964 Buick, and headed back east. I remember thinking as I drove too fast across the Midwest, "If Mom and Dad died in a car accident, I'd just take a left and head up to Canada."

I hadn't had a haircut since I left home in February. My hair had reached my shoulders by the time I arrived back in Rochester for my trip to Texas. My mother was appalled. "I cannot believe you look like that," she said. My father was also appalled, but he didn't say anything. He just looked like he didn't understand. Mom had her hair cut and got a "permanent" every month. Dad got his hair cut every two weeks. So had I for most of my life.

Lackland Air Force Base

Basic Training

My parents drove me to Monroe County International Airport on May 16, 1969, for my flight to San Antonio, Texas, and an eventual bus ride to Lackland Air Force Base. I was cleanly shaven with a short haircut. To deprive the Air Force of the satisfaction of Samsoning me, I had gone to the barbershop two days before my departure date and told the barber to "cut it all off." I wore a three-piece glen plaid summer suit. As if by appearance I could deny my destiny. In my suitcase I carried some books and a couple sets of casual clothing.

When I arrived at Lackland, I soon learned that I had not earned an exemption from the initial ritual scalping. In fact, I was amazed at how much hair the barbershop in Rochester had left, as the clippers hummed and I watched clumps of my reddish hair fall front, left, and right.

Later, we stood by our bunks to have our possessions inspected. My books caught the Training Officer and Drill Instructor's attention. *Soul on Ice* was deemed "commie propaganda," and *Paradise Lost* led to an immediate interrogation. "What's this? Pornography?" asked Technical Sergeant Hecht. All my books were confiscated.

In the morning, we were marched over to the men's clothing department to get fitted for our AF outfits. There were about fifty new recruits in my flight. After we each received a duffel bag, we were ordered to squat down in a large room opposite the clothing department. First we were fitted for our underwear.

"Everyone under 125 pounds, stand up," shouted a sergeant.

Their T-shirts and underpants were hurled at them.

"Everyone between 125 and 175, stand up."

I caught a half dozen boxer shorts.

"Everyone over 175, stand up."

Another barrage of boxers.

This sequence was repeated for fatigues, casual tan uniforms, and dress blues. They were a tad more precise with our shoes and jungle boots, but no half sizes—"Make up yer damn mind, troop!"

We marched back to our barracks lugging about fifty pounds of new gear. I guessed that the tailor would stop over later.

One night during the first week, I had an unusual dream. I was trapped in a motel room, surrounded by Marines. Buddy Kupka was with me. Alive. I was smashing the motel windows and firing wildly, determined to protect Buddy from the Marines who were closing in on us. Reveille awakened me, and the return of consciousness left me feeling surprised at the dream's details and sad that I hadn't saved Buddy. And confused because even though we had been fraternity brothers at Trinity, we had never been close to being friends.

During that first week, I learned to march, shine shoes, make my bed, wax the barracks floor, do an about-face without losing my balance . . . barely . . . , and appreciate the freedom that I had taken for granted all of my life. One morning, while standing outside of the mess hall after breakfast, my glance caught a newspaper dispenser by the door. I realized that for the first time in my life, I did not know what was happening in that big old world beyond the limits of my daily routines. In fact, I knew nothing about anything that had happened in the past ten days, and blinked away the tears that accompanied that realization.

Later, we received rather perfunctory hand-to-hand combat training. We learned to stomp on the toe of anyone grabbing us from behind, kick assailants where it would hurt the most, and crawl across the hardened Texas terrain. All in one afternoon.

Another day, we ran an obstacle course featuring all of the classic jungle challenges. We swung across a small body of water on a rope. Most of the guys purposely let go to fall in and cool off. We climbed a wooden wall while holding a rope. We ran through smoke across a covered bridge. We crawled through a pretend minefield. Summer camp games. Nothing that anyone would ever encounter in Vietnam.

Our minefield featured a half dozen wire mesh-enclosed paths across about 200 feet of dirt baked dry and hard by the summer Texas sun. The enclosures were slightly wider than our shoulders and slightly higher than our prostrate bodies. I had to keep my elbows against my sides and my hands under my collarbones when crawling. I could turn my head from side to side, but not really raise it more than a couple inches off the ground.

I was trapped. It was a potentially claustrophobic situation. And the guy in front of me snapped. He just froze up about half-way across the fake minefield and would not move. No matter how loud the sergeants yelled at him. No matter how loud they swore at him. No matter how many "mines" exploded nearby.

The guy behind me crawled up so close that his head was between my ankles. He thought I was the one who had panicked. He screamed at me just like the sergeants were screaming at the guy in front of me. I was hot and sweating and struggling to stay calm.

Eventually the guy in front of me crawled out. I followed him into the air, spat out a half-mouthful of dirt, and exhilarated in being able to run.

A couple days later, we went to the firing range. Despite all the toy guns I'd played with and treasured as a kid, I had never fired a real gun. I was handed an M-16, a state of the art rifle that fired bullets so . . . effectively . . . that they guaranteed no slight injuries. No enemy soldier would ever proudly show his son or grandson a scar where he had been grazed by an M-16 bullet. He would either talk about luck and a near miss, or wear a sleeve pinned at his shoulder. M-16 bullets explode upon contact. They blow off whatever body part they even nick.

Things were so "hot" in Vietnam that there was no ammunition at Lackland for us to use while learning to shoot. We were able, however, to practice dissembling and assembling M-16s. We were all given copies of "The M-16A Rifle: Operation and Preventive Maintenance," a 1968 Department of Defense publication that featured an informal, humorous tone and "Connie," a curvaceous blonde. On its cover, two foolishly grimacing GIs cower as bullets whiz by, and one jokes about the difference between official and combat operations.

"Connie" on page 8 of "The M-16 Rifle Operation and Preventive Maintenance" manual issued to all servicemen during Basic Training.

On pages 2 and 3, Connie smiles, holding an M-16 under the heading, "How to Strip Your Baby." "She" is "Your" M-16, and "You want to know her inside out, every contour and curve, every need and whim, what makes her tick." On page 8, Connie has changed from her civvies into jungle fatigues. She offers "tips that'll keep it your ever-lovin' . . . Sweet 16."

Her concluding advice appears on page 16 under "More Pointers to Ponder." Appealing to the combat hero illusions of thousands of American boys, and speaking in the jargon of Vietnamese citizens and soldiers picking up bits of English informally, Connie says, "For you M-16 zapsters here are some numbah one suggestions to keep you go go."

On the last page of the manual, readers are introduced to "Maggie," an M-16 magazine with arms and legs. She leans on the heading "Putting Maggie Together," winks at the riflemen-readers, and offers her advice on the four-step process for magazine maintenance.

We flipped through our manuals and then pretended to shoot real bullets. The range sergeants called it "dry firing," but it was no different than running around the house as a kid, hiding behind the maple tree and shouting "Bang! Bang! Bang! You're dead, Bobby!"

We "ready-aim-fired" all morning. The range sergeants checked the way we held our rifles and the position of our heads while aiming, and rigorously monitored where our guns were pointing every second of our practice. We were all rewarded with sharpshooter medals to wear when we went home on leave. Later, we reported for our flights to Vietnam. There our sharpshooting credentials just might be challenged.

One morning during my final week of Basic, a grizzled forty-something Army sergeant who had just returned from Vietnam addressed my flight. He had been a guard on the perimeter of Tan Son Nhut Air Base, the main Air Force base in Vietnam. It was just outside of Saigon. He told us about a friend of his who was stationed in a guard tower on the northwest corner of Tan Son Nhut, right where the Viet Cong had broken through the perimeter fencing during the Tet Offensive of 1968. He told us that if the VC hadn't paused after their successful breakthrough, they could have destroyed most of the planes on the base.

But they paused to get organized, firing everywhere at the same time. An American military policeman (MP) in his tower in the middle of the attack called in a helicopter gun ship, knowing that his body would be among the VC bodies tallied after the American firepower had won the day.

During Basic, I had learned that I would not be going to Officer Candidate School. The escalation of the undeclared war had eliminated the need for any more administrative officers. OCS was only accepting potential pilots and navigators.

Back in the first week, I had scored high on a language aptitude test, and was awaiting orders to go to Monterey, California, to learn Chinese or Russian when the Air Force made a decision that changed the course of my life. An initial draft of Palace Dog, a program to teach English to Vietnamese officers so that they could learn English prior to coming to the United States for pilot training, had been planned to be staffed by commissioned officers. When the draft yielded a much more highly educated crop of enlistees than had been anticipated, it became apparent that a sufficient supply of English instructors could be harvested from the noncommissioned ranks, saving the military millions of dollars. The program was to be staffed with enlistees who had two or more years of college.

One day we were told about the Palace Dog program and asked if we were interested in volunteering for it. Three days later, I was told that I was in it. My expectations for comfortable living on the California coast were replaced by apprehension about teaching English in Vietnam.

With a week remaining in Basic, we received "Liberty" on a Saturday morning. It was our first hours of freedom since arriving at Lackland. I ran over to the basketball courts with about a dozen other guys. I took off my T-shirt and played all morning under the bright Texas sun. My skin was scorched, but I dodged prosecution.

When Sergeant Hecht saw my sunburn, he threatened me with a court martial for destruction of government property. "Listen, boy, you belong to Uncle Sam now," he explained, and added that I could be severely punished for causing myself to be unable to execute my assigned duties.

After six weeks of Basic featuring an afternoon of hand-to-hand combat training, a full day running the obstacle course, a morning of dry firing, and daily practice marching to "hup, two, three, four," I was ready to be a soldier and go to war teaching English as a second language.

While I had been beginning Basic Training, the 101st Airborne was engaged in ten days of fierce fighting with NVA troops at Hamburger Hill in the A Shau Valley. After taking the hill, the troops were ordered by their commander to abandon it. It was the last major search and destroy mission by U.S. troops.

American troop levels had peaked at nearly 550,000 at the end of April 1968, and there were over another million primarily Air Force and Navy troops supporting those actually on the ground in Vietnam. President Nixon's Secretary of Defense Melvin Laird coined the term "Vietnamization" to denote the shifting of the burden of combat from American soldiers to South Vietnamese soldiers. In June 1969, Nixon announced the beginning of troop withdrawals. Although I didn't know it at the time, the Palace Dog ESL program that I had been assigned to was a key element of Vietnamization.

On June 27, three days before I finished basic training, the cover of *Life* magazine featured a full-face photograph of an American soldier who had been killed in Vietnam. The issue's title was "The Faces of the American Dead in Vietnam: One Week's Toll." Inside

Author upon completion of basic training, June 1969.

were photographs of each of the 242 Americans killed during the preceding week.

Casual Control

After Basic, I was assigned to Casual Control, a place and status for those who had finished Basic and were awaiting starting dates for their various technical training assignments. I was waiting for the next Defense Language Institute course on teaching English as a Second Language. I was pleased to be wearing my first stripe. I was no longer an air cadet. I was a full-fledged airman. My monthly salary increased from 40 dollars a month to 60 dollars a month, but my sunburn was still bothering me.

My friend John Hoose was in OT Hold; he was waiting for the next Officer Candidate School class to start. We had met in Rochester while taking the AFOQT, and by coincidence had been in the same flight during Basic. John had graduated from Rochester Institute of Technology with a B.S. in optics. When he mentioned to a Selective Service official in Geneseo, New York, that he was considering applying for Conscientious Objector status, the official replied, "My son is going, and I can't do anything for him, so what do you expect me to do for you." He then went to speak to an Army recruiter about being a Warrant Officer and flying Medevac helicopters. "You know how many college graduates I talk to?" asked the recruiter.

"No," said John.

"None," said the recruiter, and then he explained that helicopter pilots were the most frequently killed or wounded personnel in Vietnam.

"I'm going to Canada," John thought, on the way to his parents' house. But there was a letter waiting for him from the Air Force offering OCS and research, so John enlisted.

John and I were able to get together during our mutual free time and play bridge or basketball, catch a movie, or just hang out at one of the snack bars on base. I knew John's feelings about the war, and he seemed to enjoy spending his time with me and some of the other future teachers more than with his fellow future officers. I imagined that most of them were hawks, and I often questioned them about their perspectives on their future endeavors flying helicopters, fighters, and B-52s.

One night, halfway through a pepperoni pizza and a pitcher of beer, I asked John's roommate Bill Gehle, a future pilot, "How can you justify dropping bombs that you know will kill innocent civilians?"

"Oh, I just fly the plane," he explained. "I don't drop the bombs. The bombardier drops the bombs."

Defense Language Institute

I was freed from the limbo of Casual Control in mid-August. About thirty airmen destined to teach English to South Vietnamese officers were gathered in a single barracks on Lackland, ready to be trained to survive in Vietnam and to teach ESL. All in eight weeks at the Defense Language Institute (DLI). The first two weeks were a Combat Preparedness course, since we were going into a war zone. Our Instructor had served two tours in Vietnam. I wrote to my parents describing him as "really a great man who tells it like it is over there." I wonder how I knew.

We were all given copies of *A Pocket Guide to Vietnam*, a 1966 Department of Defense publication. On the cover was a young Vietnamese woman wearing a traditional *ao dai* (a light silk dress slit on the sides) with black silk pants and a conical straw hat, walking her bicycle. The guide's opening message was a slight variation on others we had received during our K–12 school years: "If you are bound for Vietnam, it is for the deeply serious business of helping a brave nation repel communist aggression. This is your official job, and it is a vital one, not only for the preservation of freedom in this one country, but for the survival of freedom everywhere . . . You will be helping to block the spread of communism throughout Southeast Asia . . . and the success of your mission requires that you build a good relationship with the South Vietnamese people."

The stated American mission in Vietnam was to "win the hearts and minds of the Vietnamese people." Listed under the heading

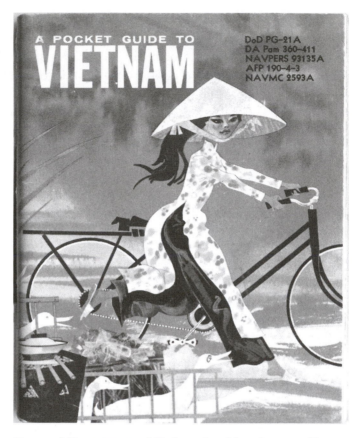

**Cover of Department of Defense booklet given to all serv-
icemen being prepared for duty in Vietnam.**

"Suggested Reading" in the back of the guide was an article from
the October 1964 issue of *Foreign Affairs* entitled, "Do We Understand Revolution?" by Edward G. Lansdale, the CIA officer referred to by some historians as the "Father of South Vietnam."

Our sergeant-instructor warned us to be careful at all times and
not to trust the Vietnamese. He also warned us about boredom,
and encouraged us to find constructive ways to keep ourselves
busy. He explained that we would be living on the sixth, seventh,
and eighth floors of the Hung Dao Hotel, an old colonial hotel in
Saigon nine miles from Tan Son Nhut and MACV Headquarters
where there were excellent athletic and recreational facilities. I de-

cided that I'd buy a guitar and fill up some of those potentially boring hours and days by learning how to play it.

On the hard, baked dirt of central Texas, we practiced "tactics" for survival in southern Vietnam, an equatorial jungle. Only the temperature in Texas was about right. We played war games in the 100-plus-degree heat of August. We moved out. We hit it. We high crawled and low crawled and recovered. And we sweated and itched.

Our pretend battlefield was covered with small burr-like nettles that had an amazing ability to stick to the skin. Every time we "hit it," our hands, elbows, and knees were pricked by hundreds of these stickers. And when we rolled over, we were covered with them. We were familiarized with M-1 and M-2 rifles, M-60 machine guns, and M-79 grenade launchers, and we reviewed M-16s. But again, we did not fire any live ammunition. Some men took this training extremely seriously. Others, like my new friends and me, felt we were enacting some crazy *Mad* magazine satire of combat preparedness. We managed to conceal our insubordinate attitudes during our training days, but we broadcast them all over the place during our off-duty time.

By chance, I found myself rooming with a crew of New Englanders. Airmen Drew H. Clarke, John T. DeFlumeri, and Lawrence Spinelli were all from the Boston area. Different social groups formed around different interests. Surprise! There were some bridge players and some poker players. Some guys who liked to talk about sports and some who actually played them. I spent time with all four cliques and became friends with two guys from Iowa.

Airmen Robert M. Gall and Robert J. Rhame were the first midwesterners I had ever known. Gall was a Cyclone—a 6' 4" graduate of Iowa State University whose stature and deep, resonant voice belied the fact that "Big G," as we dubbed him, was just a pleasant, docile kid. "BJ" Rhame was a Hawkeye—a 5' 6" nongraduate of the University of Iowa whose continuous smirk accurately expressed his cynical attitude toward the world and himself.

Big G had a college degree, but he lacked a critical consciousness. BJ had completed a year at Clinton Community College in Clinton, Iowa and then gone off to the University of Iowa where he spent too much time having fun and not enough time with his books. But he had learned a lot in his twenty years. He described an old guy he had worked with at the Clinton Corn Processing Company as someone who "knew what the world was like," and the same phrase was an apt one for young BJ.

Big G and I, and most of our DLI classmates, had been assigned to the Palace Dog ESL program, but BJ had to take a test to qualify. Air Force policymakers had decided that any enlisted men with two or more years of college would be assigned to this part of the Vietnamization program. Others would have to prove their qualifications by passing an aptitude test.

Despite the counsel of his father, who had been in the Navy, and every other veteran whom he had ever known, BJ broke the "Do not volunteer" rule in basic training. An officer had described the Palace Dog ESL program to his flight, and BJ was the only one to express interest. He had never considered "slipping off to Canada," he explained to me, but he wasn't eager to see combat either. He had been glad to hear that his test score earned his acceptance into the program. He figured that everyone going into the military in 1969 was going to Vietnam, and that being in a classroom in Saigon was a lot safer than being dropped off on a landing zone (LZ) in the jungle near the DMZ.

For six weeks after our military training, we practiced teaching ESL to Iraqi and Iranian enlisted men. They had learned English rapidly in their home countries, but were struggling to achieve fluency in the United States because they so enjoyed living here and were being so hospitably cared for by Uncle Sam—they were not in a rush to return to their home countries. Our government was paying their salaries and providing their room and board at Lackland.

To say our classes were small would be an understatement. We usually had only three or four students in our practice teaching classes. I already understood that the best method of teaching a language was oral. My Vietnamese students would learn English as adults just as I had as a child—by listening and speaking and repeating and repeating. I learned nothing from my practice teaching with the Middle Eastern soldiers, who were hanging onto their status as military trainees temporarily residing in the United States by not learning any more English.

Late in our training at DLI, my fellow future teachers and I learned that the Armed Forces Language School (AFLS) at Tan Son Nhut where we would be teaching had been hit by enemy mortars. This news certainly heightened our apprehension about our destination and what we would encounter there, but Vietnam still seemed unreal. Even though we were on a military base with little freedom, we were still living in the United States.

Long after I left Lackland, I learned that while I had been there on September 2, 1969, Ho Chi Minh had died, twenty-four years after proclaiming the independence of Vietnam. But I left Texas for Rochester and then Saigon thinking that he was still alive and President of North Vietnam.

Questions for Discussion

1. Why had the author never expected to be in the military?
2. Why did he go to Vietnam?
3. What did he know about Vietnam prior to going there?
4. What was his perspective on American involvement in Vietnam prior to going there?
5. What significant experiences had created his perspective?

Part II

A Year in Saigon (1969–1970)

Leaving the United States

I spent the week of my leave in Rochester and Hartford. Remembering the advice of the sergeant from DLI, and figuring that I'd have a lot of free time with nothing to do in Saigon, I gathered some books and then went shopping. I bought an acoustic guitar with a black carrying case.

I was rather dispassionate about my situation, but my friends and family were all overly passionate about expressing their concern for me. After spending a couple of days with my parents, I drove to Hartford to see my college friends Bob Gutzman and Bob Heimgartner. It was fun, but I realized that we were not fraternity brothers any more. We had graduated. They had jobs and wives. I was just passing time until my flight to Vietnam.

Back in Rochester, some high school friends and their parents had a going away party for me. My buddies and our dads joked and laughed while drinking beer and smoking cigars. Four moms sat together at the opposite end of the living room, whispering and looking our way.

My parents took me to the Rochester airport a day before my flight to Vietnam from Travis Air Force Base outside of San Francisco. In uniform, I checked my duffel bag and carried my guitar with me. I spent my last night in the United States in San Francisco with Jesse Brewer, a former fraternity brother from Trinity who was in grad school at the University of California at Berkeley. He took me over to Peoples' Park, the site of many antiwar demonstrations and confrontations with policemen and National Guardsmen adjacent to the Berkeley campus. The ensuing "riots," as they were labeled in newspapers and on the evening news shows, had taken their toll on the park. It was just a small city block of bare dirt, scrub bushes, and a few scraggly trees. Anything growing that had not been injured by protestors had been obliterated by phalanxes of uniformed enforcers of order—policemen and National Guardsmen. That evening, we ate spaghetti and drank some wine, and Jesse taught me four basic guitar chords. I remembered them and practiced occasionally for a couple weeks in Saigon.

I checked in on time at Travis Air Force Base, wearing my Air Force casual tan uniform, and boarded my plane for Vietnam—a Pan American Airlines 747. American servicemen—Army, Navy, Marines, and Air Force—all flew back and forth to Vietnam on Pan Am or Braniff or TWA. All of the Air Force planes and pilots were flying missions—dropping bombs, spraying napalm, and helicoptering GIs into and out of jungle hot spots—so the State Department had contracted commercial airlines to transport troops to and from Vietnam. Their corporate profits and stock prices soared.

Saigon

We landed at Tan Son Nhut, the largest U.S. Air Force base in Vietnam, in the middle of the night, disoriented by the fifteen-hour flight and the time changes. We stumbled off the plane and across the asphalt to a bus the color of our jungle fatigues—dark olive drab. The air was hot and humid and still. I flopped myself and my duffel bag into the first empty seat, and slid toward the window. There was heavy, metal mesh screening over the windows to prevent Viet Cong guerillas from tossing grenades onto the buses. The meshing made it even harder to see. As the bus rolled off of the base toward downtown Saigon, I peered out and saw people sitting on small stools or just squatting on their heels dispassionately watching the bus roll by. I could see electric fans and the glow of small television sets behind the traffic watchers. Even before the bus reached the hotel, these vague glimpses of my new world told me that my life would change, and that America would never be the same for me again.

The bus stopped in front of the Hung Dao Hotel, a nineteenth-century French colonial hotel recently converted into living quarters for American GIs. I trudged up seven flights of stairs, found Room 712, and flipped on the light switch. It seemed even hotter in the room than it had been outside despite the click-click-clicking of the ceiling fan.

Overtired, overheated, and overwhelmed by being so rapidly dropped into a strange, new world, I collapsed on the bed, pulled off my jungle boots, tossed my jungle fatigues toward a chair, and lay wide awake in shorts and a T-shirt wondering how I had landed in Saigon, and what was going to happen to me.

Before I turned off the lights, I started my journal. "What have I but words whose inability to describe 'Day one' is exceeded only by the intensity with which Saigon has bombarded my senses?" I wrote. "I will fling an M-16 over my shoulder tomorrow morning and go to school, and the worry about having too much to write has been transformed into the desperation of not being able to write. Saigon stinks and it's hot. America truly is the land of milk and honey. How will I ever be able to live there again if I learn to live here?"

When I awoke the next morning, I stepped into the bathroom and reached for the faucet. Then I remembered that we were not supposed to drink the tap water. So I dressed and loped downstairs to go to breakfast across the street on the first floor of the Khe Sanh, another old French hotel converted into billets for American soldiers.

I walked out of the Hung Dao and stopped at the curb. I stared at the Khe Sanh on the other side of Hung Dao Street, a four-lane road that ran straight into the center of Saigon. But that does not accurately describe what loomed between me and my breakfast. Sure, it was a four-lane road on those rare occasions when there were two standard-sized cars, trucks, or buses going each way at the same time. But usually it was a continuous blur and blare of two-way traffic ignoring all lane markings and featuring hundreds of motorcycles slaloming their way through a shifting maze of larger and slower vehicles—cars, trucks, buses, and military vehicles. Many of the motorcycles were driven by "cowboys," young Vietnamese males who were not in school, not employed, and not yet drafted.

This was, after all, in an Asian metropolis. Saigon had been designed by the French in the late 1800s to be a showplace of colonialism, a beautiful city of 50,000. Its tree-lined boulevards had been immortalized by the postcards and paintings of the late nineteenth and early twentieth centuries. During the Japanese occupation in World War II and the ensuing French reoccupation, Saigon grew into a city of 300,000. When I arrived in 1969, it was a city of over 3 million, and growing every day as more and more refugees from the wartorn countryside sought safety in the city. Many times on my way back to the Hung Dao after a day's teaching, I found shacks wall-to-wall along a roadside where none had been in the morning. Within hours after the announcement that an area had been opened for resettlement, refugees erected make-shift shelters built out of scrap boards and flattened Coke, 7-Up, Budweiser, and Miller cans.

Hung Dao Street, however, was one of Saigon's major thoroughfares, with stately, old five- to ten-story buildings on both sides, flanking a continuous parade of the most ancient and most modern means of transportation. It was not unusual to see a Mercedes Benz passing a cart loaded with mangoes being pushed by an elderly vendor.

Fifty-year-old trucks and cars chugged past, coughing clouds of dense smoke from the holes in their exhaust pipes. For every old truck, there were a hundred *xich los*, whose overburdened engines blared and spewed thick smoke. These brightly painted, converted motorcycles were equipped with a bench seat between two front wheels and were especially popular with GIs. At the time, Saigon had the worst low-level air quality of any major city in the world. (Today, many residents wear face cloths when riding around to protect themselves from the air pollution.)

Vietnamese families traveled on even the smallest motorcycles. It was not unusual to see a whole family pass by comfortably on a Honda 50. Dad drove with one child on his lap. Mom held onto Dad's waist and sat sideways behind him. There was usually a toddler behind her, and an older sibling on the bookrack. The typical 1960s American family was a husband and wife and two kids traveling to a Little League game in the family station wagon. The typical Vietnamese family was a husband and wife and three kids traveling to the market on the family motorcycle.

There were pedicabs, too. Leftovers from the precolonial era, these were still being driven by wiry middle-aged men to help their fellow citizens avoid long walks in the equatorial heat or the monsoon downpours. Sometimes the weight of a GI, however, was too much for even the strongest pedaller. I often saw GIs pedaling their "drivers," who sat smiling broadly at their temporary change in status.

So, I was still on the Hung Dao side of the street, mesmerized by the kaleidoscope of traffic, but getting hungrier by the minute. I took a couple steps off the curb and hopped back quickly as a

Xich lo, a converted motorcycle with a seat in front for passengers.

motorcycle zoomed around a battered old Ford. As I rationalized that I wasn't really hungry and let the urgency of my need to cross the street subside, I looked to my left, toward downtown, and saw a young Vietnamese girl with her left arm holding a younger brother and her right arm similarly encircling the waist of an even younger sister. She was gracefully drifting across the street, stepping warily here, pausing there, and miraculously seeming not to be in danger. She reached the other side and continued calmly on her way uptown as if neither the weight of her two siblings nor the chaotic traffic were problems.

As a proud young athlete, I accepted the challenge. If that Vietnamese kid, that girl, could get across the street, then so could I! And cross the street I did! But neither as quickly nor as gracefully as she had.

Some of my AFLS classmates were also staying at the Hung Dao, but BJ and Big G were staying at the Saint George Hotel in Cholon, the Chinese district of Saigon. At first it seemed like they were in

Author's friends and fellow English instructors Robert J. Rhame ("BJ"), *left*, and Robert M. Gall ("Big G") walking outside MACV Headquarters.

another city, but I soon figured out how to get there by scheduled military buses or hailing a *xich lo*. I much preferred the latter.

The Hung Dao only had guest rooms. Each was assigned a "mama san." An Americanism that originated in Japan at the end of World War II, "mama san" became a universal term for any Asian woman who performed housekeeping chores. In Vietnam it referred to women between the ages of twenty and sixty who made beds, cleaned rooms, washed and ironed clothes, and shined boots for about 5 dollars a month. The Saint George, by contrast, was a full-service hotel. In addition to its ten floors of rooms, there was an outdoor basketball court, a restaurant and a bar on the first floor, and a room of slot machines on the second floor.

In my room at the Hung Dao, for a couple weeks I practiced the guitar chords that I had learned on my last night in the United States. I also practiced yoga that I was learning from a book I had bought. I'd start out with the basic, introductory exercises. I relaxed and sensed my feet . . . my ankles . . . my calves . . . my knees . . . and I usually fell asleep. Soon, however, I was spending a lot of time and my money at the Saint George. In late November, I sold my guitar and packed away the yoga book for good.

The school where I would be teaching was on the perimeter of Tan Son Nhut, about fifteen miles from the center of Saigon. It was about a half hour by bus, *xich lo*, or Vespa van from the Hung Dao. Even at six o'clock in the morning the air was heavy with humidity, and there was almost never even a slight breeze to lessen it.

On my fourth day in Vietnam, I wrote the first of fifty-eight letters to my parents: "Dear Mom and Dad—Where do I begin? With the traffic? The poverty? My accommodations? Or the knowledge that America will never be the same for me?"

My first excursion into Saigon was on the following Sunday with BJ. There was continuous traffic accompanied by the continuous noise of honking cars and trucks and exhaust roars of hundreds of motorcycles. And an acrid smell of smoke.

The first floor of every building in Saigon was a store. On the curbside of the sidewalks, there were wagons of all sorts and tables arrayed with goods. Everything was for sale on every block of every street. Soda, coffee, or tea. Hot beef, pork, or chicken. Marlboros, Winstons, or Salems. Fried rice, steamed rice, or sticky rice. Oranges, papayas, or lychee nuts. Coconuts with straws inserted to drink the juice or cracked open to scoop the meat out of. Lacquered bracelets, boxes, and pictures. Buddhas of all sizes carved from wood, marble, or jade. Plastic, wooden, or lacquered chopsticks. Even rubies, emeralds, and diamonds. Gold and silver. Dishes and cookware. And clothing and fabric in all colors and patterns.

Everything was priced, but none of the prices meant anything. I did not know until that first day's walk that I had grown up in a fixed-price economy, but that most of the world operates on a bargain-based economy. Many an American paid many a dollar more than he had to because of this fundamental market misunderstanding.

BJ saw a vase that he liked. "*Bao nhieu* [How much]?" he asked.

"Seven hunna p [700 piasters]," replied an elderly woman.

"I give you 350," he countered.

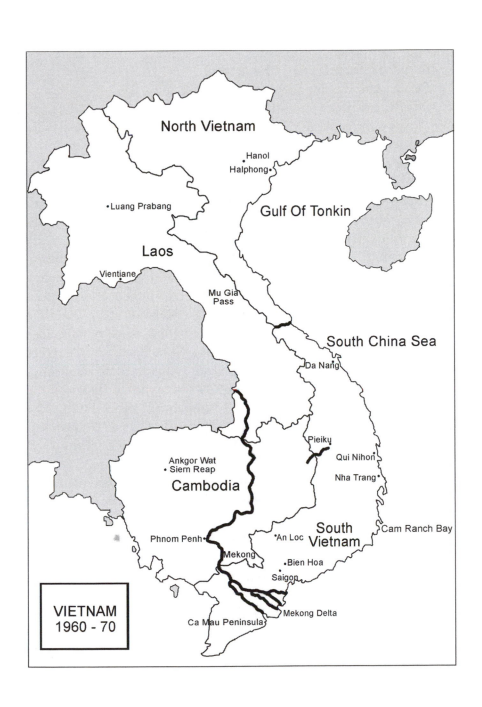

North Vietnam

Hanoi•
Halphong•

•Luang Prabang

Gulf Of Tonkin

Laos

Vientiane•

Mu Gia
Pass

South China Sea

Da Nang•

Pieiku•

Ankgor Wat
• Siern Reap

Qui Nihon•

Cambodia

Nha Trang•

Cam Ranch Bay•

Phnom Penh•

•An Loc

South
Vietnam

Mekong•

•Bien Hoa

Saigon•

Mekong Delta•

Ca Mau Peninsula•

VIETNAM
1960 - 70

"No, no. Tee tee [too little]," she protested.

He turned, and started to walk away, but she shouted, "Four hunna."

He turned back. "Okay," he agreed.

"Okay," she repeated and wrapped up the vase.

After hours of strolling the sidewalks, BJ and I decided to eat. We purposely looked for Vietnamese restaurants where there were no American soldiers. We could have gone to a number of clubs for servicemen or a number of Vietnamese restaurants that catered to Americans, but we wanted to be in Saigon, not an American oasis in Saigon. We wandered away from the center of the city, out toward the Saigon River, and found a small restaurant off the main street.

Fortunately the menu was in Vietnamese and English. BJ ordered a genuine Vietnamese dish. I ordered shrimp fried rice, a daring venture for a guy who had grown up on meat and potatoes and green beans. I had never even eaten pizza until starving late one Sunday at Trinity. There were only chopsticks at our place settings—no knives, forks, or spoons. When our meals were served, I was starving and staring at an enticing plate of shrimp, rice, and vegetables. I tried desperately and awkwardly to get the chopsticks to pick up a shrimp. I had one, but it slipped off before I got it into my mouth. Abandoning my goal of dexterity, I picked up my bowl and used the chopsticks to politely shovel the food into my mouth as I had observed others doing.

One day, I ate lunch with an artilleryman in from the field on a three-day pass. Authorized breaks for soldiers in Vietnam included three-day passes "in country," usually to a big city for the infantrymen living and fighting in the countryside, and one-week "R and Rs," rest and rehabilitation trips out of country, usually to Thailand or Australia. He called all American soldiers "grunts" and spoke matter-of-factly about daily atrocities and "those bastard Montagnards" (tribesmen living in the mountainous Central Highlands). When I described my duty of teaching English to South Vietnamese officers, he smiled and told me that I'd better appreciate my "skate job," a slang expression for an easy job. He was in his third day in Saigon and heading back into the mountains that evening.

Economics

In just six months, I received a second promotion. I started out as a no-striper, an Airman Basic. At the end of Basic Training, I was promoted to Airman and got to sew a stripe onto my sleeves. In November, I was promoted to Airman First Class. I was a two-striper.

More important than the stripes, of course, were the raises that accompanied each promotion. As an Airman First Class, my salary nearly doubled to 112 dollars a month. I got another 100 dollars a month because I was working in a place where American soldiers were getting killed. That extra hundred was called "hazardous duty pay." Even though Congress had never declared the American military action in Vietnam an official war, it had authorized combat pay for all military personnel on duty in Vietnam.

This was quite a bonus for guys like me living safely in Saigon, but not quite fair compensation for the hundreds of thousands who were living in tents in the jungle, never knowing if they would ever get to spend a dollar of their combat pay.

My lodging at the Hung Dao was provided, of course, and I received a food allowance of 50 dollars a month. I paid 27 cents for breakfast, 45 cents for lunch, and 60 cents for dinner at the Khe Sanh across the street. I could also eat at any of the clubs around Saigon. At the club on the top floor of the Plaza Hotel, I could get a grilled cheese sandwich for 20 cents, a hamburger for 25 cents, a cheeseburger for 30 cents, a basket of fried chicken for 80 cents, or a T-bone steak for $1.75. All sandwiches came with French fries, and nonalcoholic drinks were free.

So, for 40 cents I could get two grilled cheese sandwiches, two orders of fries, and two iced teas. Beer and alcohol were also cheap. Budweiser, Miller, and Schlitz were 15 cents a can. Cigarettes—Marlboros, Winstons, Salems, and Kools—were only 10 cents a pack. All the clubs also had rooms of slot machines.

Pulling the bandit's one arm, listening to the whirring wheels, I was thrilled to have a chance to win some money, and ached to see 7-7-7 spin to the center row. I wonder who was pocketing all of the money picked out of the pockets of the foolish, bored, young men who threw too many of their too few dollars away in those rooms.

We didn't use real money—neither coins nor green dollars. We used Military Payment Certificates (MPC). It was all part of the American effort to bolster the South Vietnamese economy and keep American currency out of the hands of the enemy.

Vietnamese money was called either dong or piasters. The international exchange rate was about 400 Vietnamese dong for one American dollar, but when American GIs exchanged their MPC for Vietnamese money to spend in local stores or restaurants, they only got 118 Vietnamese dong per American dollar. So the U.S. government burdened its lowest ranking employees with building the South Vietnamese economy. And we were constantly exhorted to take the moral high ground and not deal on the black market. There the exchange rate for MPC approached the international rate. For green money it doubled. Anyone could double his money by exchanging green dollars for MPCs, but green money was illegal. We were not allowed to have any American currency. In the early 1960s, GIs would take their paychecks to banks and buy money orders, and then take those into town and exchange them on the black market. That ploy was stopped when banks and post offices were ordered that any purchased money orders had to be mailed (out of the country) immediately after being issued.

BJ was outraged by the inequity of being drafted, sent to Vietnam, and then being robbed, as he saw it, to help Vietnam—a country that made the news for its governmental corruption as often as for its conduct in the war. So BJ took his bought-on-the-black-market pistol and his cashed paycheck of about 100 dollars and went downtown to get himself what he considered a fair exchange of Vietnamese money.

BJ from Clinton, Iowa, was a mediocre poker and bridge player, but an excellent raconteur. He later returned for a second tour at AFLS and was the last instructor to leave Vietnam in 1973.

A guy showed him a roll of Vietnamese 500 piaster bills, and BJ looked first at him, and then away to make sure no MPs were strolling nearby. Then BJ handed the guy his 100 in MPC, and took the roll of Vietnamese bills and stuffed it in his pocket, suppressing a big smile all the way to a bar. He sat down in a booth toward the back, pulled out the roll of bills, took off the rubber band, and unrolled a single 500-piaster bill wrapped around about 50 one-piaster bills. He'd been had. During his quick lookaway, the Vietnamese guy had switched rolls on him.

As his anger subsided, BJ acknowledged, "Those guys were professionals. I tried to check that roll but those rubber bands were on so tight it would take a machete to get 'em off." Eventually we became wiser. We made contacts whom we trusted. We bought cigarettes and liquor and sold them for two or three times what we paid for them at the Base Exchange (BX). We learned how to earn our fair currency exchange rates. One night in the middle of my year in Saigon, I drove off MACV with a duffel bag full of cartons of Salems, Marlboros, and Kools on the back of my Honda. When I passed the guard station, my heart was pounding.

I read about the horrors of the black market in an article in the *Stars and Stripes*. About how the GIs were helping the enemy by their black market activities. It described a cache of Viet Cong weapons and money that was found near Bien Hoa, about twenty miles north of Saigon. The VC there were killing Americans with M-16s, and they had over 5,000 dollars in green money, all in hundred and 500 dollar bills. No GI ever had a 500 dollar bill. Only the officers were making enough money to be tossing that stuff around.

I had learned of my school being attacked during the 1968 Tet Offensive while I was still at Lackland. Although I knew that random guerilla strikes occurred in Saigon, I never really worried about dying in Vietnam. My perspective was detached. I understood the sort of random possibility of being killed, but I did not ever feel that I was in danger. I now see that my attitude was like that of Paul Baumer, the narrator of the World War I classic *All Quiet on the Western Front*. He recognized that the older soldiers had started lives that were interrupted by the war, but he and his peers, all young men in their twenties, had left their homes and parents and had not yet connected to anything else. They were no longer children, and not yet adults whose lives had meaning. They were the "lost generation" portrayed in the stories and novels of Ernest Hemingway.

My initial days in Saigon changed my perspective. I wrote in my journal, "At first I was worried about dying, but now I'm worried about living." But that attitude soon changed, too. If I was going to be in Saigon, I decided to live in Saigon.

Armed Forces Language School

After initial processing, I spent Wednesday, October 29, at the Armed Forces Language School (AFLS) observing a teacher who had been teaching for four months. I expected to do the same for the rest of the week, but when I reported to work on Thursday, I was assigned my first class. I was completely unprepared. I did not even have a copy of the book my students were using. But I taught all day. I talked and talked, and explained and explained. And stared out at a dozen blank faces.

My students said I was difficult to understand. "If you talk slowah and cleeah, Missuh Cowah, we can maybe unnastan you," pleaded one student, Mr. Minh. That night I was disheartened.

Then Friday saved me. It was as encouraging as the day before had been discouraging. I slowed down my speaking, enunciated more carefully, and waited for students to repeat words or answer questions. Smiles appeared on the blank faces of my students. That night I wrote in my journal, "Now I know what it is to be a teacher. Thursday I was frustrated. Tonight I'm smiling, and looking forward to tomorrow."

Fortunately for me, that first class was a 2400-level class. These were advanced level students who could communicate very well in English. All of them were "Aspirants"—Officer Candidates. If they passed their examinations at the end of two weeks, they would go to the United States for pilot training.

There were three phases in the AFLS curriculum—Elementary, Intermediate, and Advanced. At the completion of each phase, students took English Comprehension Level (ECL) examinations consisting of fifty oral questions and fifty written questions. The Elementary phase consisted of four one-week courses—1100, 1200, 1300, and 1400. To move on to the Intermediate Phase, a student had to score 30 or higher on his ECL phase test. The Intermediate

Phase consisted of two two-week courses—2100 and 2200. To move on to the Advanced Phase, a student had to score 50 or higher on his ECL phase test. The Advanced Phase also had two two-week classes—2300 and 2400. To graduate from AFLS and qualify for pilot training in the United States, a student had to score 80 or higher on his ECL exams. Students were expected to become fluent in English in three months.

Our students were not really beginning speakers of English, however. All AFLS students in 1969 were South Vietnamese officers or Aspirants. Most were second lieutenants just out of OCS, but some were first lieutenants. There were a few captains and majors who had spent time in combat before their assignments to AFLS. One special class consisted of colonels and generals.

All of the younger officers had studied English in high school, and many were drafted out of college or graduate school, where they had been continuing their studies. I had many students who had been taken out of medical school or law school. Their English instruction, however, had come from Vietnamese teachers. In most cases, their reading and writing abilities far exceeded their speaking and listening abilities. It reminded me of my own foreign language education. I could read and write French fairly well, but if I accidentally tuned in a French language radio station from Canada, I couldn't understand a word. And the few times I tried to speak French, no one understood me.

Our students needed to speak English while flying—to communicate over radios. Oral fluency was the program's main goal. I spoke, and they repeated. I asked a question, and a single student answered. Then the whole class repeated his answer or my correction of it.

All of the AFLS students lived in what was called "Tent City," just behind our school and on the grounds of Tan Son Nhut. They had no space or privacy; about twenty men lived in each open-sided tent. They slept on mats that they rolled up each morning so that the wooden floors could be swept.

In comparison, we teachers were living in luxury in old French hotels in Saigon, and later in our new barracks at MACV. The barracks were all virtually brand new two-story cabins that held about fifty GIs. There were partitions separating two-man rooms from each other. We always had more space, more comfortable beds, and better living facilities than our higher-ranking students.

There was a . . . well, it wasn't really a snack bar and it certainly wasn't a restaurant as those words denote certain types of eateries in the United States. There was an open serving area with servers behind a counter providing *pho* (the beef and noodle soup that is the favorite Vietnamese breakfast), tea and coffee, and baked goods. It was just inside the fence between the school and Tent City. The entrances on both sides were monitored by armed Vietnamese soldiers twenty-four hours per day, and the student-officers had to show their identification cards when passing either way.

We were warned to be extremely careful with our M-16s. We were not supposed to lose them. We lived with them. Carried them to school each day, into each class, and home at the end of the day. We were told that some students might be Viet Cong, however, and they would grab a rifle in a second if they thought they could get away with it. I've always had trouble keeping track of my keys and wallet, and I really didn't want to lose my M-16, so at the beginning of each course, I selected one of my students to take care of it for me. I'd hand him my rifle in the morning, and he would give it back to me at the end of the day. This did not impress the real soldiers who were in charge of this platoon of English teachers.

When I first arrived, we taught on two split shifts, five days a week. The A shift was from 7:00 A.M. until noon and then 5:00 to 7:00 P.M., and the B shift was from noon to 5:00 P.M. and then 7:00 until 9:00 P.M. In late November, our schedules changed. The new shifts were 7:00 A.M. to 1:00 P.M. and 1:00 until 7:00 P.M., six days a week.

On my second Monday in Saigon, I was assigned a new class. I had just been subbing for the last three days with the 2400 class that I had been surprised to take, and now I had my first class. At the break, my former students saw me and all came over to ask why I was not still teaching them.

During my first month or so, things went well at work. I quickly came to enjoy teaching and learned by experience how to effectively help my students develop language proficiency. I was also determined to learn some Vietnamese. I asked my students to give me some instruction, but they just wanted to teach me slang and philosophical idioms. When I learned about a Vietnamese language class at MACV, I enrolled.

Things were not going so well away from school, though. There was no live TV. Everything, including news and sports, was taped in the United States and sent over. I had always enjoyed watching baseball, basketball, football, and other sports on TV back home, but for some reason I was not interested in watching games that I had already read the results of in the *Stars and Stripes*, the military's overseas newspaper.

There were a half dozen movie theaters in Saigon, but all they showed were first-run Chinese movies or old American movies dubbed in Vietnamese. There were no U.S.-operated theaters at MACV or in Saigon showing current American movies in English. And there were no pool rooms or ping pong tables in the Hung Dao, the Saint George, or the Plaza. Getting out to the facilities at MACV was a long ride from the city, and at first I wasn't even sure what bus to take.

BJ and I spent a lot of our time and money drinking those 15-cent beers, smoking those 10-cents-a-pack Marlboros, and tossing coins into the slot machines. I had written in my journal after about a week and a half, "I now know all of the ways not to spend my free time here." But it was easier to write that than to do anything about it.

One night, while smoking and playing the slots, I developed what I thought was a fantastic pronunciation drill. All of my students had great difficulty learning the difference between short and long vowel sounds. Standing at a machine, flipping away quarters—each one worth a grilled cheese with fries and iced tea—I ran through the alphabet and thought up all the pairs of words that would illustrate the effect of the "silent e" ending. I came up with "fat" and "fate," "her" and "here," "bit" and "bite," "not" and "note," "cut" and "cute," and many others.

The drill actually worked. I don't mean that all of my students immediately became exemplary orators, but most of them did begin to make at least slightly different sounds for "rat" and "rate."

I probably tried to quit playing the slot machines twenty times before my Vietnamese classes and MACV League basketball games finally enabled me to walk away from them. And I'm sure that BJ and I tried to quit smoking a hundred times. Once, after laughing at our many half-hearted efforts, we decided to run ourselves to the brink of death. We skipped lunch, changed into T-shirts, shorts, and sneaks, and started jogging laps around the two-mile perimeter of the MACV Annex. We ran about ten miles and staggered into the shower room in our barracks. I had always enjoyed long showers, but this one was a record breaker. Toweling off, we were both surprised at how good we felt, so we decided to light up a couple of Marlboros.

On the morning of November 15, the beginning of my fourth week in Vietnam, we had a meeting before our first classes. A "reactionary force plan" was presented. Our Army supervisors expected us to be ready to use our M-16s for something more than just symbolic deterrence. Ten teachers were assigned to secure the school's perimeter in case of attack. Another sixteen were assigned to form a strike force to counterattack. My responsibility was to sit in front of a classroom and "control the students." We had often been warned not to trust any of them because they could be Viet Cong or communist sympathizers.

That morning briefing rekindled memories of the 1968 Tet Offensive described to us in Basic. I also learned about the legendary AFLS teacher who ran into a closed door and knocked himself out during the mortar attack. His head was bruised. As a result of his "combat injury," he was awarded a Purple Heart, the only teacher ever to be so honored.

We were released early that evening to break the pattern of our buses rolling out of the gate at the same time every day. But contrary to the morning warnings and the apprehension of two colleagues who always rode on the back of the bus with their magazines in their right hands ready to "lock and load" at the first sign of danger, we were never hit.

We were visited by some military and Congressional VIPS and

an eighteen-member Air Force Advisory Team just two days later, though. They observed classes, interviewed teachers, and prepared a report for President Nixon. As a key part of Nixon's Vietnamization program, AFLS had to succeed in teaching Vietnamese officers to speak English fluently so that they could go to the United States for pilot training and eventually take over the missions being flown by Americans.

I was immersed in my teaching, asking questions and correcting my students' pronunciation when an Air Force colonel stopped in my doorway. Nearly a month into my teaching career, I barely noticed his presence, and continued with my lesson.

We wore jungle fatigues and jungle boots all day every day. Even when off duty, we had to wear our uniforms. We were in the middle of a war, after all. Our jungle fatigues were lightweight versions of the standard olive drab color that all U.S. soldiers have been wearing for a century or more. We had short-sleeved shirts and balloon pants that were supposed to be bloused around our boots. But the heat and humidity in Saigon were so consistently high that we usually got away with taking off our fatigue shirts and teaching in our white T-shirts.

There I was, in my sweat-soaked white T-shirt with scraggly hair and one jungle-booted foot on the table in front of the room, questioning, speaking slowly with emphasis, and enjoying it. After observing my class for about ten minutes, the colonel moved on to another room.

Then a photographer appeared in the doorway, accompanied by one of our school supervisors. "Coward, put your shirt on, they want a picture," he barked.

"Yessir," I replied, reached to the back of the chair, grabbed my fatigue shirt, and continued teaching.

"Coward," the sergeant said, and motioned me to get my foot off the desk.

Thinking, "Of course, sir, we want it to look natural," I assumed a more teacherly posture and continued my work on past tense verbs.

The photographer snapped about a half dozen shots and then moved on. I imagined my picture being on the cover of *Time*, and remembered my dreams of having my picture on the cover of *Sports Illustrated*. I concluded my sixth letter to my parents with, "Keep your eyes open, maybe I'll be on the cover of the next *Time* you grab out of the mailbox."

At dinner one evening, I sat down at a table and eventually got talking with a Navy forespotter, a guy who goes out on his own to call in targets to his main boat. He talked of gore and whores. He had been in Vietnam for eighteen months and was in Saigon to "re-up"—volunteer to stay in Vietnam for another six months. When asked about his perceptions of the Vietnamese people, he muttered, "Personally, I hate 'em all."

In mid-November, Big G mentioned that he had had his elementary class write autobiographies. He showed them to me, and I copied excerpts into my journal. One student had written, "I long to return to my natal land, gloriously. God! When will this dream come true?"

Another had described his ambivalence about his involvement in the war. "I could no longer be passive, but had to support my country. But why must we kill each other? We are all Vietnamese. Where is the compassion, the brotherhood?"

Their words resonated with my own thoughts, and I decided to have my students write about their lives, and not just the post offices, restaurants, libraries, and zoos in the lessons in our text books. I assigned autobiographies to one class, had another write "Thank you" notes to my Mom for some goodies she had sent, and had a third express their perspectives on the war in their homeland.

Almost every time my students wrote, most of them mentioned experiences or thoughts about their pasts, presents, and futures that were not explicitly asked for by the directions for their assignments.

"Before and now, I'm not marry, but many times my plan was to marry and no success because the war destroyed it," wrote Tieng, who was resigned to studying English "to go to the U.S. and I will learn to be a pilot."

Sang had recently graduated from high school. He wrote, "I hope in the future, end war, and I shall continue studying."

If I interpret Ly's draft accurately, he shared Sang's aspirations for all of his contemporaries. "I wish my country shall no more war, because many people died in years ago. Certainly if no war, they're doctors, mechanics, instructors . . . I am very sad for my country," he concluded.

That Sunday, I was having lunch at the Khe Sanh across the street from the Hung Dao, and two Army guys sat down at my table. They were from the 108th Transport Support Group in Long Binh, about twenty miles north of Saigon. The Corporal was a supply clerk and the Private First Class was a truck driver. They were eager to share their war stories.

"One guy drove the Saigon route two days, had two accidents, and quit," reported the driver. "There aren't many guys who can drive this route."

"How about Battson?" interrupted his sidekick. "Him and me bring two deuce and a halfs down and have to stay overnight, right? Coming back, I'm riding shotgun and our shotgun is sittin' in the middle. Typical Saigon traffic. Big deuce rollin' along, horn blowin'. Some gook on a bicycle got his handlebars caught in the ribs of the front tire. His bike flips up in the air and lands under the rear wheel. His leg's there, too."

"Did you stop?" I asked.

"Hell, no, we didn't stop. Those fuckers'd kill you if you did. Of course if the QC [Vietnamese military police] or the white mice [Vietnamese civilian police] fire, you stop. If you keep rollin' for two shots, your truck will be drivin' itself after the third."

I don't remember the exact date, but about two months into my stay in Vietnam, I realized that the kid who had been afraid to cross the street had become a young man living in Saigon, one of the most colorful and exciting cities in the world. It was an oasis in the midst of the horror going on in the countryside from the Mekong Delta to the DMZ.

While my fellow American soldier-teachers spent their off-duty hours either enjoying American amenities on the base or in the clubs in Saigon or snapping pictures of beggars downtown on Sunday, my friends and I got hooked on Chinese movies and were

Typical movie theater marquee. Here, the Hung Dao Theater on Hung Dao Street, just a block from the Hung Dao Hotel, author's first billet in Saigon.

proud to be learning to eat with chopsticks in Vietnamese restaurants.

I enrolled in a Vietnamese language course at Tan Son Nhut. Two nights a week, I returned to the primary role of most of my life, student, but with one significant difference. While marking time in high school and college, I had rather passively played the game of getting grades, now I was very actively striving to learn to speak and understand Vietnamese. I listened carefully to our teacher (a Vietnamese major), took neat and thorough notes, and spoke clearly during drills. I began breaking up my teaching days by practicing my Vietnamese with my students. Soon I was speaking so well that their laughter occasionally subsided and silent stares of near comprehension appeared on their faces.

I became fascinated by the little details of our cultural differences. I marveled at the deeds of the mythical Chinese movie heroes who were able to leap from the ground to the roof of a neighbor's house, and catch darts between their fingers and return them to their assailants. My students were similarly thrilled by the deeds of mythical American cowboys who could shoot pistols out of the hands of robbers and murderers while riding horses at breakneck speeds.

I learned to love fried rice. My students all craved French fries.

I challenged them with tic tac toe, and then became embarrassed by its simplicity after my students taught me *ca ro*, a more challenging extrapolation of the principles involved in lining up Xs and Os. *Ca ro* is played on graph paper, and the winner must get five Xs or Os in a row, unbounded by his opponent's marks. Unlike tic tac toe, there are no ties or stalemates in *ca ro*. There is always a winner, even if the paper needs to be extended in a certain direction. The better the players, the longer the game takes.

My students were awed by all of the things that Americans owned, and I was awed by their happiness despite all of the things that they did not have. When I remembered that the calendar was flipping pages toward the holidays, I felt sadder about not being home for my parents than for myself.

Holidays

Thanksgiving

I celebrated Thanksgiving in 1969 a little differently than I had celebrated it in my first twenty-two years. There were goodies, of course, but they were not mixed nuts, mint wafers, trays of veggies and dips, and assorted cheeses and crackers. My students and I celebrated with Hostess Ho Hos, Pepperidge Farms Goldfish, and crumbling caramel brownies and chocolate chip cookies. They had been sent by my Mom. Undaunted by the geographical distances and climatological differences that separated us, she bought and baked and packed up a box of goodies just as she had often done when I was a mere 100 miles away at summer basketball camp or 300 miles away at Trinity.

I had taught these Intermediate Phase students for four weeks, and they were going to take their ECL phase tests soon, so I took half my bounty to class. We had a party and discussed Thanksgiving, Native Americans, and my parents. As a writing exercise, I had them write "thank you" notes to my mom the following day.

Again, their amusingly enigmatic natures emerged in both their enjoyment of the treats and in the recurring themes of their letters. They were too easily pleased by sweets for adults . . . soldiers . . . officers. They all looked forward to going to America to learn to be pilots, but in fascinatingly passive, apolitical ways. For example, they had no idea how big the country was. In fact, they all wrote about expecting to meet my parents who lived in Rochester while they were in pilot training programs at Lackland Air Force Base in San Antonio.

These young men all knew who they were, though, and had strong feelings for their country. They longed for peace. And they appreciated their instructor's interest in learning their language.

Regarding the treats, the class's perspective was most eloquently expressed by Tran. "My roommates and I thank you very much for your cookies, and chocolates which Mr. Coward gave us to eat in the classroom. I hope that you will send the candies and cookies more and more again!"

Regarding their futures, Van wrote, "If we study and we speak English very well, we will go to America. Over there we will learn to fly the airplane and we will become a pilot."

And when they had a little time off, they all wanted to visit my Mom and Dad. "I'm eager to go to the U.S. very soon. I'll come to your house if I'm free," wrote Dao, as if my parents lived just off the base.

Seven students began their "Dear Mrs. Coward" letters by stating, "I'm Vietnamese." One continued by adding, "I want to write about my country for you . . . I intend for Mr. Coward to tell you stories about Vietnam."

Students who I had mistakenly assumed were more concerned with their morning break than with their personal and historical situations showed me otherwise. Thanh expressed his thoughts about the past and the present. "The population's life is very poor because the war has destroyed in many years . . . The Vietnamese people also hated the war and they hope the peace returning."

Tran's gaze was focused on the future. "I expect, my country have a long peacetime, one day."

Some spoke clearly and some spoke ambiguously. "I hope to meet you and your family in the United States in order to tell you about Vietnamese War," wrote Nau.

"Sometimes Mr. Coward likes to study Vietnamese," noted Chau, who then exaggerated, "He speaks Vietnamese very well."

This latter courtesy stood in marked contrast to the predominant American instructors' tendency to ridicule their students for not mastering English in three months, despite their own inability to pick up even the simplest Vietnamese phrases in the same time. Most of my fellow teachers' repertoire consisted of "mama san," "dinky dau" (actually *dien cai dau*—"crazy"), "di di mau" ("go fast—get outa here!"), and the famous "number 10" (slang for "very bad").

Chau continued, "I think that Mr. Coward stays here (in the Vietnam) more long time. He will become Vietnamese." Classmate Tin warned my mother, "You will wonder when Mr. Coward comes back home with speaking Vietnamese."

Phan Ba Tien knew that I was homesick, because he was too. "I decide him very homesick. Why I know Mr. Coward home sick? Because I have family very farther and my family have eleven persons . . . and every year I have 15 days to come back visit my family."

On the first Sunday after Thanksgiving, we moved from Saigon out to MACV. Washington was sending more and more troops to Vietnam, and more and more barracks were being constructed out at MACV. Our new location would place us just a short half-mile bus ride from our school.

A row of newly constructed two-story barracks at MACV Annex where AFLS instructors lived.

We were moving from distinguished colonial hotels into Wood Shop 101 structures tossed together with the least wood and metal possible. They were large two-story cabins with common sinks, toilets, and showers at the end of rows of about twenty beds on both sides of center aisles. Partitions broke up the beds on both sides into two-person rooms. Each floor of each building had four mama sans assigned to it.

My great enjoyment of playing basketball at the Saint George, even in fatigues and jungle boots, rekindled my lifetime love of the game, and I got into a league at MACV. Play was even better than it had been on the Division III circuit in New England. Somehow, every outfit knew who played, and the ability to shoot jumpers or dribble well probably saved quite a few guys their lives. And cost some nonplayers theirs. Every soldier who was processed into Saigon on the way to a field assignment who had played high school or college basketball got assigned to a desk job in Saigon so that he could play for his outfit's hoop team. Every team's roster had former Division I players and schoolyard legends from every big city in the U.S.

My enjoyment of teaching continued. There were no more dramatic swings in perspective like on those first two days of terror and triumph. My political perspective was different. It kept changing based on my experiences and the news of the war. One day I was horrified by Pham's tale of having American soldiers break into his home outside of Hue and point their M-16s at his father and mother, brothers and sisters. One pointed his M-16 at Pham and screamed, "You VC! You VC!"

While his parents and siblings sobbed and trembled, Pham insisted, "No VC! No VC!"

They were spared, but I wondered how he could be so friendly with his American teachers after their countrymen had treated his family so brutally.

Another day, after reading in the *Star and Stripes* about peace demonstrators in the United States carrying Viet Cong flags, I was furious that they didn't understand that VC were killing their former high school classmates. I even found myself lapsing into the rationale that had been used to justify the bombing of Hiroshima and Nagasaki. Proponents of those attacks argued that killing over 150,000 Japanese in two days actually minimized the total number of casualties that would have resulted from an invasion of Japan. Our government and the military claimed that if the Americans left Vietnam, there would be a bloodbath as North Vietnamese troops marched south and murdered South Vietnamese soldiers and civilians. So I was thinking that if American troops were not in Vietnam, even more people would be dying than there were with our support of the South Vietnamese.

When the United States withdrew its troops in 1973, however, the North Vietnamese did march south, but they did not slaughter their former adversaries.

At the same time that my political thinking was riding a roller coaster, cultural differences were catching my attention and causing me to question some aspects of progress. Riding from Saigon to MACV and back every day, I studied the changing streetside scenes. I saw toddlers walking along narrow planks down at the port, and marveled at the fact that they did not fall into the river and drown. And I saw elderly men and women, and marveled at the fact that they were still walking to the market each morning.

I thought about how protective American parents are of their infants, often following them bent over to catch them if they fall when learning to walk across the living room. And I remembered my two grandfathers' spending their final years alone. One was in a state-operated care facility after a cerebral hemorrhage. He escaped, temporarily, in the middle of winter. He bolted out the front door wearing only a hospital gown, and ran as far as he could through a foot of snow, right into the woods behind the building. He didn't know his sons' names any more, and he didn't know how to get home, but he knew he didn't want to live in that building.

My other grandfather was in an expensive private facility. He just sat on the side of his bed staring at the wall. His last words after every visit were, "I hope I die tonight."

I realized that no Vietnamese grandfather lives alone in a public or private institution. They all live with their families, and their families take care of them.

A Day in the Country

Since we carried M-16s to class and had them with us at all times, we were taken out to a firing range in the countryside one Saturday morning to see if we could hit anything. They loaded us up in a big olive drab bus and took us out of Saigon. We left the city's paved roads and rolled over rural dirt roads. I saw jungle for the first time in my life. It was even greener than I had imagined as a young reader, or seen on movie screens.

Two young Vietnamese boys were leading a water buffalo pulling a small cart loaded with bananas. They smiled and waved. We shouted to the bus driver to stop, dropped our M-16s, and grabbed our cameras. We took their pictures.

At the firing range, twenty of us lined up about half a football

Two young boys driving water buffaloes and a cart transporting bananas in a rural area south of Saigon.

field from a corresponding line of human-outlined targets with "kill" spots highlighted. This time we were given live ammo. We "locked and loaded," as if preparing for . . . "combat" . . . "a fire-fight" . . . "engaging the enemy."

I peered through the sight, aiming just above the center of the "head" because we had been instructed to allow for the slight effect of gravity. I fired. There was no "kick" like the legendary knock-you-down-if-you're-not-prepared-and-tough-enough ones I'd read about in books and seen in movies when boys were learning to shoot and become men.

I fired a clip . . . 20 rounds . . . 20 bullets. I had no idea whether I hit my target, or the piles of sand behind it, or the palm trees far beyond the sand piles.

"Good pattern, son," drawled the sergeant from the range. "Where'd you learn to shoot?"

"I've never fired a gun before in my life, sir," I answered in amazement.

I shuddered, but I was also proud. I always tried to be good at whatever I did.

On the way back to Saigon, BJ asked to see my gun. "Hey, there's no firing pin," he blurted.

"Bullshit! How do you think I was shooting all morning?" I replied.

"Well, there's no firing pin in here. Take a look," he said, and handed it back to me.

I had forgotten what I'd learned in Basic and couldn't figure out how to find the firing pin. Holding up my firing pin and elbowing Big G, BJ was dying with laughter at the kid from the East who had just shot a gun for the first time in his life, impressed the lifer sergeants with his shot patterns, and still didn't know how to take his M-16 apart.

Merry Christmas

Christmas ambushed me. No decorations. No snow. No shopping. My excitement was simply because it was an extra day off, a week away. After spending Christmas Eve smoking Marlboros, drinking Budweiser, and pouring quarters into the slot machines, I awoke late Christmas morning.

My parents had sent me a check for 20 dollars, and I told BJ that I'd buy him a steak. He had helped me through many a financial crisis during my battles with the one-armed bandits.

Before I left my room, I looked over all the Christmas cards I had received. I felt a twinge of guilt. Ever since my arrival, I had been overwhelmed by mail. I got letters from my Mom almost daily. I also got letters from friends from high school and college. And I got letters from parents of my friends and friends of my parents. I never responded to most of them other than to write, "Thank the Burrells, Uncle Fran and Aunt Donna and Mrs. Snipes for their recent notes" in my letters to my parents.

Mom and Dad's Christmas cards were my favorites. I thanked them in a letter, writing, "Compliments to you both. Of all the cards I received, your two were by far the best. They spoke a universal language saying feed each child, spare it from disease and give each man the possibility of hope, for nothing more exists."

BJ and I went to the Plaza and ordered T-bone steaks. Since we were dining early, we had iced tea and, of course, baskets of French fries. The club was decorated with Christmas lights and a few fake trees, but you can't fake winter so close to the equator. I knew I was enjoying a day off, but I was not really convinced that it was Christmas.

After our holiday feast, we walked over to the USO. Soldiers and civilians were hosting a party for Vietnamese orphans. Many of them had lost their parents in the war. Some had lost parts of their bodies. My attention was caught by a little girl about six years old. She was eating a single scoop of vanilla ice cream with a plastic spoon out of a plastic cup. She looked like she was the happiest person in the world.

I wondered how a scoop of ice cream could bring such joy to a child who was missing her left leg. I wondered whether this party would leave more pleasure or pain in the hearts and minds of these children. I was uncomfortable because of the one-day wonders being bestowed on these orphans by GIs who seemed more proud of their do-gooding than sympathetic toward the children. I got BJ's attention and said, "Let's go."

We played some basketball back at the Saint George, showered, and then had another Christmas dinner in the mess hall. This one was turkey with iced milk, the only way to get it cold in Saigon. Someone had posted a sign over the entrance that read, "You will have a Merry Christmas and a Happy New Year—General Orders."

After filling myself with turkey and mashed potatoes and stuffing and gravy and maybe even a few green beans, I went to the library and read for a while. Back in my room later, I polished off four small bottles of booze (airline samples) that my Uncle Bud and Aunt Dot had sent me. Happy Holidays!

1970

After Christmas, I got the profile change that I'd been pursuing ever since I started to get a rash after shaving. I went to the infirmary, and a doctor gave me some ointment and a shaving waiver. I carried it with me everywhere. It exempted me from the requirement to be clean-shaven at all times. For a while, everywhere I went away from the barracks or school, I got stopped by officers who challenged my appearance.

There were basically two kinds of officers stationed at MACV. Some just over from the United States didn't understand the differences between Saigon and West Point. Others who had been in Vietnam for a while understood that in some sense the difference between officers and enlisted men was less important than the fact that we were all in Vietnam. There were still supervisors, though, who were more concerned with appearance than performance.

After I got over the anxiety of thinking that even though I had permission to have a beard, I was still maybe going to get in trouble, I began to really enjoy the privilege. Back from school and off duty, I'd put on my one-piece Puregro coveralls with the collar up and the Peanuts cartoon that I'd drawn on the back. And I'd put my shades on, and stroll right into the heart of MACV Headquarters to buy a bag of chips or mail a letter or just wander around.

One day, I came around the corner of a building and saw a young lieutenant who looked about twelve years old coming out of the post office, so I drifted off to my right, walking aimlessly off the sidewalk and across the parking lot.

"Hey, you," he shouted.

Obviously I was not an officer. I kept strolling.

"You," he shouted again, as he marched toward me.

I slowed and turned toward the lieutenant. I had not yet seen

The author in January 1970. A shaving waiver allowed him to have a beard.

Taxi Driver, so I hadn't learned to snarl, "You talkin' ta me?" I just took my waiver out of my front pocket, unfolded it, and handed it to him without saying a word.

He looked at the paper, handed it back to me, and sputtered, "Were you tryin' to avoid salutin' me, airman?"

"No, sir," I answered and gave him a less than snappy acknowledgement of his superior rank.

"That's better," he snapped as he returned the salute, "but don't let it happen again."

I got my stamps and bought a copy of *Sports Illustrated*. I was headed back to my barracks when I noticed a crowd gathering around a volleyball court. Six American officers were taking off their hats and dress shirts on one side of the net, and six Vietnamese officers were doing the same on the other side.

The Americans were all white guys, about 6' tall and 180 pounds with three-quarter-inch brush cuts. The Vietnamese were all about 5' 4" and maybe 110 pounds, with jet black hair that flopped from side to side as they warmed up. I decided to stick around for a while and watch what would assuredly be an annihilation.

The Americans won the coin flip and elected to serve first. When the two teams took the court, the American server was appropriately standing one step behind the end line and his teammates were standing exactly in their designated spots on the court. The Vietnamese were sort of milling around in the center of their side of the court. It just didn't seem fair.

The server slowly drew his right arm back and served underhanded, just as he and I and every American kid had learned in gym class, popping the ball over the net toward the middle of the opponents' side. This sparked some surprising activity among the Vietnamese players. All six were immediately moving. One crouched low and set the ball to his right. A teammate came flying though the air, but just faked a spike that had the Americans all moving to their right. Even before the decoy had landed, a teammate soared and slammed the ball down just inside the Americans' left sideline.

It was not a fluke. The Vietnamese played a different game than the Americans. The Americans served underhand to put the ball in play. The Vietnamese served overhand to win points. The Vietnamese played in the air and occasionally landed, while their foes played on the ground and occasionally jumped.

I had been right about the outcome, but wrong about the winners. The Vietnamese won quickly and convincingly in three straight games, yielding only a few points each game.

And I had thought that bigger meant better.

By the middle of January 1970, I was beginning to lose some of my enthusiasm for teaching. I had spent three months with all levels of classes and had not had a break. Admittedly I was spoiled. Throughout high school and college, I had always enjoyed extended holiday breaks, and even though I worked summers changing tires and making deliveries, that, too, was a break from school. There was no homework, and after dinner I played basketball and then hung out with friends.

We had changed from our split-shift schedules to the single-shift schedules of 7:00 A.M. to 12:00 or 1:00 P.M. to 6:00, but that entailed an accompanying change from five-day weeks to six-day weeks. Sunday just didn't seem like a weekend. I was looking forward to Tet in early February. We would have four days off. Of course, there was a little anxiety sitting right next to that excitement because in 1968, just two years earlier, the North Vietnamese and the Viet Cong had selected Tet as the start of their strongest attacks of the war.

An addition to our school that would double its size was being built, so I knew that neither my teaching duties nor the flow of students was likely to decrease. My fifty-three-year-old Mom was home vacuuming, ironing, and cooking meals for my Dad, but Vietnamese women her age were the school's construction crew. All of the men were in the military, I guessed. These elderly waifs—I bet there wasn't a single one who weighed over 100 pounds—were wielding pick axes and shovels, digging the ditches for the foundation of the addition. They worked in the heat and humidity twelve hours a day for about 50 cents a day.

Part of my diminishing interest in instruction was because I had just been assigned a 1300-level class of enlisted men. They were an addition to the AFLS student population. They needed to learn English to be trained as mechanics for the different planes. There were no technical terms in Vietnamese for the systems and parts in modern aircraft. Lower-level classes were always the most difficult, and these students seemed neither very sharp nor very motivated.

I was still enjoying my Vietnamese course, though. It met on Wednesday and Saturday evenings from 7:00 until 9:00. Those days were especially long ones since I was on the afternoon shift and didn't get back from school until 6:30. No time for dinner. Just enough time to walk over to class.

One day at lunch before leaving for school, I met another Army infantryman in Saigon on a three-day pass. This particular corporal was down from Da Nang, just south of the DMZ. I had heard about friendly fire incidents in which Americans either got lost in the jungle or called in air support that misfired on its own troops, but this man's tale really shook me.

Just a week earlier, he and four others had been out on patrol south of the DMZ in dense jungle. They had been alerted by radio that enemy troops were in their vicinity. So they set up an ambush. There were only five of them, but they each had an M-16, and two had M-60 machine guns. Two others had M-79 grenade launchers. They waited silently.

When the troops who they expected to be North Vietnamese entered the ambush, the Army troops opened fire. They killed two U.S. Marines and injured another six. The trapped Marines killed one and injured four of their U.S. Army attackers before both sides realized that they were on the same side. This firefight had lasted less than ten minutes.

Ridin' with the Cowboys

After five months in Saigon, I had to get my own wheels. I went downtown one Sunday and ordered a Honda 55, a hot machine. Police had bigger bikes, but no civilians or soldiers were allowed more than 55cc-engine cycles.

I had ridden a smaller Honda that a friend had back in the summer of 1967 in Rochester, but I had barely learned to ride it by the time the summer was over. When I went to pick up my brand new silver-and-red bike in Saigon, I realized that I had forgotten how to ride one. A salesman gave me a wonderful demonstration of how to shift using my foot and hand, but he explained the process in Vietnamese and demonstrated the steps so fast that I couldn't quite get it all.

And I was not sure how to get to MACV, either. I sputtered and stalled a few times, and eventually got out into the flow of the traffic. As I approached a major intersection and saw that there were no traffic lights or signs, I stopped and stalled again. I was paralyzed. Drivers were honking and zipping by me on both sides as I stared ahead in terror at the continuous flow of motorcycles, cars, and trucks zooming and swerving through the intersection in both directions.

I got my bike started and sat there for what seemed like an hour just revving the engine in neutral. I looked left, and then right, for the opening in the traffic that never appeared. Curfew was approaching. I didn't want to spend a night in jail. Off I lurched, stopping twice more, offering apologetic looks to the Vietnamese who barely avoided hitting me, before making it across.

When I got to the base, I parked the Honda, found BJ, walked over to the NCO club, and inhaled a beer while telling the tale of my ride. He laughed even louder than he had when he tricked me by removing the firing pin from my M-16.

Within two weeks, I had mastered my new Honda and learned my way around the streets of Saigon. I was ridin' with the cowboys. At the few intersections where there were traffic lights, cars and trucks lined up in the two or three available lanes, but all of the cowboys zigged and zagged up to the front. Each light change signaled the start of a race.

Depending upon the traffic, anywhere from twenty to a hundred bikes would be jammed together in front of the cars and trucks that had stopped for the light. Each driver sat balancing himself and his bike with his left foot on the pavement, right foot on the gear lever, and his right hand revving the engine. Green! We popped our clutches and roared off.

I loved it. I wasn't the fastest bike in Saigon, but I sure wasn't the slowest, either.

In addition to racing the other cowboys, there were times when I'd race the rain. Vietnam has two seasons—a wet season and a dry season. The wet season is three months of monsoons. These storms come out of nowhere, strike suddenly, flooding streets and drenching anyone caught outside, and then vanish, leaving only blue skies and water in the streets.

One afternoon, I made my first dash downtown trying to beat the rain. I could see ominous black clouds rolling in from the east but figured that I could cover the ten miles before the storm arrived. I was about halfway to Saigon when the first drops hit me. They stung. Traveling about forty miles an hour into the wind and rain blowing toward me made each droplet feel like a knife prick. Soon, however, the stinging was replaced by an absolute drenching rain that soaked me to the skin in about thirty seconds. When I pulled into the Saint George and got off my bike, I shook myself off like a dog. Inside BJ's room, I took off my jungle boots and emptied about a quart of water from each one into the shower drain. Then I took off my clothes and wrung each piece out like my grandparents had when they washed their clothes in the late 1800s.

My slow class finished its month of Beginning level work. When I first met them, I had set a goal of getting half the class to pass the ECL and move onto the Intermediate Phase, but eleven of the twelve students passed. They were elated at their results but sorry to leave my classroom. "When you began to teach us, we could not talk, and now we have all improved greatly. You are our benefactor," commented Hoang.

I picked up an Advanced class the following Monday. These guys were stars. Except Lieutenant Thanh. He smiled a lot, but seldom spoke and had conspicuous trouble with "th" sounds. His "fifth" was "fiff," and his "the" was "za."

His friend Phan was the top student in the class. He was outgoing, and his pronunciation was excellent. He was supporting Thanh as well as possible. One Saturday, Phan asked me to join him and Thanh for lunch the next day. We went to a very expensive restaurant downtown, and I was not allowed to even leave a tip, let alone buy a round of beers. Walking around the city after lunch, they offered to buy me bracelets and watches.

"Which one you like, Mister Coward?" asked Phan.

I corrected his grammar—"Which one *do* you like?"—and politely refused. "No, thank you."

We went to Thanh's house for dinner. It was surrounded by walls, and the entrance was guarded by an armed, uniformed soldier. The interior was exquisite, beautifully furnished and decorated with ornate lacquered wooden pictures of the four seasons and Vietnamese legends. Thanh's father was a general, and his mother mentioned that she had been shopping Saturday. In Hong Kong. She added that if I'd like to travel with the family on its next visit to Hong Kong, I'd certainly be welcome.

Phan was our interpreter. Thanh just smiled. Neither of his parents spoke English. Following an elaborate eight-course meal served by a half dozen servants, I expressed my gratitude for the family's hospitality, but declined their invitation to accompany them on their next shopping excursion. On my way back to MACV, I realized that the entire day had been designed to get me to pass Thanh so that he could go to the United States.

As the course progressed, I learned that Thanh's tongue was unnaturally short. It barely reached his teeth, and that physiological fact explained all of his pronunciation difficulties. Mr. Thanh

Author enjoying a Marlboro on the second-floor porch of his MACX Annex barracks prior to reporting for guard duty as a rifleman with C Company in the spring of 1970.

never made it to the United States, and I never shopped with his family in Hong Kong.

In mid-April, I received a note to report for training for perimeter guard duty. Mr. Coward, English teacher at the Armed Forces Language School, became Airman First Class Coward, Rifleman with C Company. Every fourth day for two months, I was on duty from 6:00 P.M. until 6:00 A.M.

We had to get into formation—lined up and standing at attention—by 6:30 P.M. Then we were given any pertinent information about anticipated action and dismissed to our barracks. We did not patrol the perimeter of the base, but we had to be available to do so in case of an alert or an attack.

C Company went out to the firing range in the country for another half day of target practice. As perimeter defenders, we were also introduced to the M-79 grenade launcher. It didn't launch hand grenades, those small pineappley, pull-the-pin, count-to-ten-and-toss bombs that had been used since World War I. It fired fat bullets, about two inches in diameter and four inches long. It was short, like a sawed-off shotgun. I broke it, and inserted a shell. I closed it. Click. I pulled the trigger. Whoosh. Boom. And ten or twenty enemy soldiers about fifty meters away would have been killed or wounded.

We were support troops who would be called on in case of an attack like the 1968 Tet Offensive. That lone Saturday I had fired at targets in front of banks of sand in the midday sun, but we were being prepared for night duty, and the perimeter of Tan Son Nhut and MACV Headquarters was primarily a bustling urban neighborhood.

I was terrified by the possibility of having to actually shoot at people. My stint, however, was uneventful, and in mid-September, I was awarded a Certificate of Service for my work with C Company ensuring the safety of my fellow soldiers at MACV and my fellow Americans back home.

At the same time that I was called to perimeter guard support duty, we were in a period of heightened security at school. Teachers alternated extra morning duty for a week at a time, arriving at school at 6:15 A.M. to check the rooms for bombs.

MACV was never attacked or even fired upon during my year there, and our school enjoyed an equally tranquil twelve months. My only confrontations were with supervisors over incidents like my wanting to throw a football around at a time when the school was expecting a VIP visitor.

At the beginning of our half-hour break, I strolled into the school office to get the football.

"Anything we can do for you?" asked Sergeant Smith.

"No, just gettin' the football," I replied.

"No, no, no. We've got a colonel comin'," said Smith.

I put the ball back and mused aloud, "That's interesting."

Leaning back with his feet on the desk, the sergeant inquired, "What's so interesting?"

I remarked, "UCMJ [Uniform Code of Military Justice], huh? No football allowed during breaks when an officer visits the school to see typical activity?"

"No, no UCMJ. Just Tech Sergeant Harry P. Smith says 'No.' That should suffice."

I walked out and muttered, "It doesn't, but it does," realizing that my boots had better shine, my pants had better be bloused, and I'd better not be a minute late for school or a class until Tech Sergeant Harry P. Smith had completed his assignment at AFLS.

My Lai

Sometime in March or April, I picked up a copy of the *Stars and Stripes* and saw the first published pictures of My Lai. In my journal, I recorded my hope that my students would not see these pictures.

On March 16, 1968, a platoon of 150 soldiers led by Lieutenant William Calley had been ordered into combat by Captain Ernest Medina. It was a typical search and destroy mission. Their objective was the Son My village in the hamlet of My Lai. Expecting to encounter Viet Cong soldiers, but meeting only civilians regarded as Viet Cong sympathizers, Calley and his men killed hundreds of unarmed, defenseless Vietnamese men, women, and children.

At dawn, six Hueys had dropped Calley and his men into position. They marched into the tiny hamlet where just days earlier they had been giving away candy and cigarettes and getting water from the residents, herded the villagers out of their huts, lined them up, and began firing. By noon over 500 had been killed.

Helicopter pilot Hugh Thompson was flying above My Lai and observed the killing. He landed directly in the line of fire between the troops of Calley's Charlie Company and the fleeing Vietnamese civilians. He ordered crewmen Lawrence Colbourn and Glenn Andreotta to shoot any American soldiers who continued to shoot the Vietnamese villagers. After radioing for assistance, Thompson began rescuing injured and surviving Vietnamese.

An Army cover-up began immediately. It was reported that the My Lai operation was an important defeat of Viet Cong forces in one of their primary bases of power. A *Stars and Stripes* feature applauded the courageous efforts of the American soldiers who had risked their lives. Commander in Chief Westmoreland sent a letter of congratulations to Charlie Company.

Army Colonel Oran Henderson's April 1968 "Report of Investigation" stated, "The area [of My Lai] has long been an enemy stronghold . . . All persons living there are considered to be VC or VC sympathizers." He further reported that the results of the operation were "128 VC soldiers KIA [killed in action] and 20 noncombatants were killed during the preparatory fires and ground action," and "U.S. forces suffered 2 KIA and 10 WIA by booby traps and 1 man slightly wounded in the foot by small arms fire."

In conclusion, Henderson reported, "The allegation that U.S. forces shot and killed 400–500 civilians is obviously Viet Cong propaganda." But many people knew what had really happened. A year later, Ronald Ridenhour, a former serviceman, wrote a letter to Congressman Morris Udall describing the events of My Lai and forwarded copies to thirty other prominent government officials, including President Nixon.

Two investigations were ordered immediately. Before their official results were released, however, details were leaked to the press, and an interview of Calley by freelance journalist Seymour Hersch put My Lai on the front pages of newspapers and magazines around the world.

"My Lai was an appalling example of much that had gone wrong in Vietnam," wrote Colin Powell years later in his autobiography, *My America Journey*. He had been a major serving in the Army in Vietnam at the time of My Lai.

Thompson and Colbourn were immortalized for their efforts in Vietnam's War Remnants Museum when it was set up in 1975. Much later, they were honored in their homeland. On Friday March 6, 1998, thirty years after My Lai in a ceremony by the granite walls of the Vietnam Veterans Memorial on the mall in Washington, D.C., Army Major General Michael Ackerman said, "This afternoon we will finally recognize these men for their heroic actions . . . that clearly capture the essence of Army values."

When the addition to our school was completed, it doubled its size. More teachers were arriving, and more students were coming, too. Classes of enlisted men had been added to the classes of officers. The enlisted men, however, were not studying to earn tickets to the United States. They would just maintain and repair the planes of the South Vietnamese Air Force, all provided by the United States.

Accompanying the addition to the size of our school and the increase in its student population was an addition to our duties. Since there were not enough MP guards to man the gate and bunker at the school entrance, teachers were assigned guard duty once every three weeks. There were a few John Wayne types who looked forward to the duty and perhaps a little action, but most of us realized that we had not been prepared for combat. Hey, we had only dry-fired at Lackland and spent one Saturday morning with live ammunition firing at targets in the Vietnamese countryside. We had played war games, but we were not ready for the real thing.

When my first turn came, I tried to get comfortable sitting on sand bags in the bunker. I listened to the radio and sang along to "Raindrops Keep Fallin' on My Head" and "Bridge Over Troubled Water." I thought about the sergeant's story about the MP who called in the helicopter gun ships on the corner of Tan Son Nhut near our school. And I tried to imagine firing my M-16 at attackers.

I knew that an attack was possible. Just a week earlier, a grenade had been tossed at the guard post outside the entrance to the Khe Sanh. It blew the guard across the street, but somehow it did not kill him. I had been in the area and started to rush over to see what had happened. Then I remembered the warnings about guerilla strikes designed to draw crowds, and the follow-up grenades or mortars directed at the assembled crowds. So I stayed away.

We were alerted to expect another VIP visitor. Secretary of State Laird was in Saigon and would probably visit our school with the Commander in Chief of the Air Force soon. This is another indication of the AFLS's role in Nixon's Vietnamization program. Frequent visitors. Additions to the facility and increases in students and staff. From the very start, I thought that the program pushed too many students through too much material too fast.

I was often surprised by the students who passed the exam and earned their tickets to Texas. Then I learned that they had developed a complicated method of cheating. A group of ten students planned to each memorize 10 questions. One student memorized 1–10, the next 11–20, and so on. Then they composed a hundred-line poem. The first word of each line began with the letter of the correct answer to that numbered question. I'm sure there must have been some remedial or review English classes developed at Lackland to support some of the students whose poetry was better than their English. The ploy was discovered, and the test was changed. I don't think a second epic poem was ever written.

In late March, I received a package from the American Red Cross. I guess someone in Rochester had gotten names of local boys in Vietnam and arranged to send them some treats. I passed out the hard candy and cookies to my students at the time, and they were thrilled. I tossed the wrapping toward the wastebasket in the corner of the classroom.

At clean-up time, the students are supposed to take all trash and dump it into the appropriate containers outside. The students in the morning class in the same room placed the wrapping paper with my name on it in the butt can (for cigarettes) and it was discovered by the Officer in Charge (OIC) of the school. Interpreting the UCMJ, he determined that two weeks of working all day would be fair punishment for my crime of not properly disposing of "critical printed material." I was to report to work for the morning shift and spend it emptying butt cans and doing other menial chores, and then teach my normal afternoon shift.

Well, the big wheel's underling, the Non-Commissioned Officer in Charge (NCOIC) of the facility, talked the OIC into only a week of punishment. When I pointed out to him that I had actually not committed a crime, he said that I could take my case to the commander of AFLS if I wanted to, but that he would probably restore the original two-week punishment.

So I swallowed my righteous indignation and dragged myself out of bed at 6:00 A.M. every morning. I didn't actually do much, just emptied all of the butt cans about twice a day. I read two books in the first three days of my sentence, and caught up on some letter writing the next three days.

On my last day of extra duty, I was in the break room by myself when a Vietnamese civilian worker at the school bowed from the doorway. His skin was dark, wrinkled, and weathered. He carried an old Budweiser can with its top cut off, and as he arose from his bow, he pointed toward the water cooler.

I nodded to say, "Of course, you are welcome to some water."

He filled his can, bowed his gratitude to me, and left the room.

Kent State

In addition to the story and pictures of My Lai, there were two other *Stars and Stripes* articles that I remember vividly. One was about a peace demonstration in Washington, D.C. I can still see the picture of hundreds of thousands of people on the Mall from the Capitol to the Lincoln Memorial demonstrating against the continuing American involvement in Vietnam.

And I'll never forget reading about National Guardsmen killing four students at Kent State University. Somehow, that hit me harder than any of the details of the war that I was seeing and hearing first hand every day. I had seen American soldiers on their way home with bandaged heads, empty sleeves safety-pinned to their shoulders, even legless in wheel chairs. And I had seen the even less fortunate maimed and disabled Vietnamese. Filthy, dragging themselves along the sidewalks of Saigon, begging.

Four Kent State University students had been killed and nine others injured by U.S. National Guardsmen on May 4, 1970. The news was in the May 5 issue of *Stars and Stripes*. A day later, I wrote about it in my journal and then in a letter to my parents. In my journal, I wrote:

> It seems the campuses in America are more dangerous than the streets of Saigon. If an American soldier over here did what the National Guardsmen did at Kent State, he would be court-martialed for murder in about two seconds. And this is a war zone. We are repeatedly briefed that even if fired upon ... even if bullets are zinging at you ... Take cover! Do not return any enemy fire unless the enemy is clearly distinguishable. In Hue [Vietnam's imperial capital, a city in central Vietnam inland from Da Nang and the scene of the heaviest fighting during the 1968 Tet Offensive], American soldiers

must call in to get permission to return fire even when attacked.

In my letter home, I asked my parents, "How did you react to the killings at Kent State? First, claims of a sniper, and then a General admits that there is 'no such evidence.' What is happening?"

Years later, I visited Kent State University and learned the details of the afternoon that made it clear that the conflict overseas had divided Americans at home, too.

On Friday, May 1, Kent State students organized a demonstration to protest the invasion of Cambodia. This action had been ordered by President Nixon because North Vietnamese soldiers and Viet Cong were repeatedly striking American troops in western Vietnam and then retreating inside the sanctuary of the Cambodian border.

Demonstrators buried a copy of the U.S. Constitution to symbolize its death, and announced a second meeting for Monday, May 4, at noon. During the evening, a crowd marched through the center of Kent. The mayor declared a state of emergency and called Governor James Rhodes for assistance. He immediately dispatched a National Guard officer who led police using tear gas and riot gear. They herded the demonstrators out of town and back to campus, quieting Kent by 2:30 A.M.

On the morning of Saturday, May 2, students assisted with the clean up of downtown. But that evening, more than 1,000 demonstrators surrounded the Army Reserve Officer Training Corps barracks on campus and set it on fire. Firemen were called to the scene but left after their hoses were punctured or cut by the demonstrators. The National Guard cleared the campus by midnight.

Sunday, May 3, began calmly, but the town of Kent and the Kent State campus were conspicuously occupied by National Guardsmen. Adding to the potential for chaos were hundreds of people arriving from out of town and out of state, either to join the demonstrators or just to see what was happening. That evening, a crowd gathered at the Victory Bell. When the crowd did not disperse, the Ohio Riot Act was read and tear gas was fired.

The demonstrators reassembled downtown, believing that an official would arrive and address them, but no one arrived. At 11:00 P.M. the Riot Act was read again and more tear gas was fired. The day ended with the demonstrators determined to hold their previously planned rally, and the National Guardsmen determined to prevent them from doing so.

By noon on Monday, May 4, nearly 3,000 demonstrators gathered on the campus commons. When ordered to disperse, they chanted, swore, and threw rocks at the Guardsmen. Tear gas canisters were fired, but had little effect because of strong wind.

Leveling their rifles with their fixed bayonets, Guardsmen marched forward, forcing the demonstrators to retreat, but the Guardsmen halted when they recognized that the crowd was not dispersing and that it was trapped on an athletic practice field fenced on three sides.

Another exchange of tear gas and taunts and rocks ensued. The Guardsmen retraced their march, followed by the demonstrators, some as close as fifty feet, but most trailing by 150 to 200 feet. At the crest of a hill on the campus, twenty-eight Guardsmen fired more than sixty shots in thirteen seconds. Kent State students Allison Krause, Jeffery Miller, William Schroeder, and Sandra Scheuer were killed. Nine other students were injured.

Kent State President Robert I. White closed the university. There were demonstrations at over 400 colleges across the United States following the killings, and more than 100 colleges cancelled their classes, sent all students home, and did not hold graduation ceremonies for their classes of 1970.

The Kent State demonstrations were a response to the American expansion of the war into Cambodia. Throughout the war, both regular North Vietnamese forces and irregular Viet Cong forces and supplies had moved from the north to the south along the Ho Chi Minh Trail, a network of paths and trails and dirt roads through the dense jungle of central Vietnam. Planes flying over the area could not even see the troops on foot or the trucks rolling south because of the density of the jungle.

When they were spotted or met in combat, North Vietnamese and Viet Cong would just drift west across the Cambodian border. By not following them, U.S. soldiers were simultaneously honoring Cambodian neutrality and allowing Cambodia to grant sanctuary to enemy soldiers. On April 30, President Nixon authorized America soldiers to pursue them into Cambodia, a policy change that meant an escalation of the war.

About a month after the incursions into Cambodia and the Kent State deaths, I was having lunch in a club in Saigon and overheard a conversation between a U.S. Information Agency (USIA) corporal and an Army enlisted man sitting at an adjacent table. They were both on three-day passes from Cambodia.

Until that afternoon, I had always read without questioning the daily casualty reports. Every day the military released the numbers of Americans, enemies, and noncombatants (civilians) killed in action (KIA) and wounded in action (WIA) during the previous day's hostilities.

But as I listened to the conversation at the next table, I realized how imprecise and occasionally fabricated those numbers were. The USIA corporal was talking about how difficult it was to estimate enemy casualties. Of course, I thought, they don't leave the bodies of their dead and injured out there to be counted by American support troops the following day. The corporal explained that they look for traces of blood on the ground or on the leaves of bushes. A little blood equals one enemy wounded. A lot equals one enemy killed. A puddle, still wet, was considered to equal two or three killed.

Continuing his explanation of his work, the corporal explained that, of course, there have to be more enemy casualties than American casualties. Especially in the Cambodian situation. Otherwise it could never be justified. He didn't use an equation that could be written on a chalkboard and taught to his successors, but he did, he admitted, always add a few to the enemy numbers and subtract a few from the American numbers.

Politics

A Lesson

I passed the midyear point quite comfortably living in Saigon. Sometimes I almost forgot that thousands of my peers were slogging around in the jungle getting sick, injured, maimed, and killed. Through my study of Vietnamese and my practice of breaking up my teaching days with conversations and lessons from my students, I gained an understanding of their perspectives on the world and their cultural values.

I'd talk about the American culture that was not in their language texts. We struggled to cross the Pacific Ocean of misunderstanding that separated us even though we were in the same small classroom.

Early lessons had focused on movies and food. Today's lesson was going to be on politics.

I wrote "democracy" and "communism" on the board.

Pronunciation was our first step.

"Day-mow-crahsee," said Tuan, stressing the "crah," but combining it with the final syllable.

"De-mah-crah-see," I said slowly, overemphasizing the accented second syllable.

"Day-mow-crah-see," said Pham, putting the stress in the right place and getting the right number of syllables.

I settled for comprehensibility without pushing for mastery. We moved to "communism."

"Co-moo-nee-zim," said Hai, stressing the third syllable.

"Cah-myoo-ni-zim," I said, stressing the first.

I had been taught that democracy was the best form of government, but I appreciated Churchill's perspective that, "Democracy is the worst possible form of government . . . except for all the others."

I knew we were in Vietnam to "make the world safe for democracy," as President Woodrow Wilson had announced in the 1920s, and to "win the hearts and minds" of the South Vietnamese while helping them protect a developing democracy. I had learned that in school, in the newspapers, and on the evening news.

I had also learned that communism was bad. It was a totalitarian system of government that denied its citizens all of the freedoms and rights enjoyed by Americans. I wanted to see how my students' knowledge compared to mine. I was looking forward to moving from pronunciation into a discussion of the differences between democracy and communism, capitalism and socialism, competition and cooperation, and theory and practice.

I soon learned that not a single student understood the principles of democracy or communism. They were all adults taken out of grad school, law school, or medical school, and assigned to the military so that they could become pilots. They were the educated elite of South Vietnam, but they lacked the political and economic understanding that I had expected. Or the English fluency to articulate them. I wondered how strongly these young men were committed to building a democratic South Vietnam . . . or fighting communism.

I moved the lesson from politics into a less conceptually complex area.

"Who are your heroes?" I asked.

"Hay-row?" answered a half dozen voices.

"Heroes," I repeated, and wrote the word on the board.

"Great men," I continued, "like George Washington and Abraham Lincoln and the Beatles and Pele."

They struggled to comprehend.

I talked about leaders and singers and athletes.

"Ho Chi Minh?" whispered Anh.

"Yes," immediately and louder, "Ho Chi Minh," agreed Quyen. Faces lit up. Smiles. Nodding.

They all agreed. These twelve South Vietnamese officers all revered one man. Leader of the Viet Minh. Proclaimer of Vietnam's independence. Communist. Recently deceased leader of North Vietnam.

Ho Chi Minh.

The enemy?

I had other surprises, too. Perhaps it was foolish to think that there would be more human commonalities than cultural differences between my students and me. Once, while writing sentences on the board to practice changing tenses, I wrote, "Do you think about your future?"

After checking to see if my students could change the sentence to the present progressive—"Are you thinking about your future?"—I returned to the original question and asked students for their answers. One student answered, "No, I don't think about my future," and a classmate concurred. I was astonished. I was obsessed with my future. Would I ever see combat? Where would I be stationed back in the United States? What would I do when I got out of the Air Force?

In a later class, however, my students revealed deeper thoughts about their future in their writing than they had in that simple grammar exercise. I had them explicitly address war and peace and the prospect of American troop withdrawals. Almost all of the students perceived the war to have started twenty years ago, during the First Indochina War. That number also corresponded to the third line of the popular song *"Gia Tai Cua Me,"* which lamented twenty years of civil war following a thousand years of Chinese rule and a hundred years of French colonialism.

Some students did not understand the war, as indicated by Hao's question, "Now let us ask ourselves for who are we fighting?" Or were his words a rhetorical question for the Americans? Others had learned the same lessons that I had learned in my schools. Long explained, "Everybody know that we can't live with the communists because they don't respect our free life of each person. A person believe to the God. They never accept it. Therefore if we want peace arrive with us, my personal opinion is we must fight the communists."

Tam was more concise, "It is war of free world and communism."

Some thought the war would end within a year, but others expected it to continue for a decade. Their expectations regarding

One of the author's advanced classes sitting around the flagpole at AFLS.

American withdrawal were similarly diverse. But they all hoped for peace. Khiem said it most eloquently. "I think one day the North people and the South people of Vietnam will combine into one block and Vietnamese people will live together in happiness."

Despite my interest in learning more Vietnamese and more about Vietnam, my enthusiasm for teaching was fading. At the same time that I enjoyed the respite of a seven-student class in late May, I noted in my journal, "My patience is waning in the classroom."

Two weeks later, I had regrouped. I had been assigned a 2100 review (repeater) class. They had all failed their ECL after two weeks of 2200, so now they had to repeat a month of work. Many seemed to be simply victims of ineffective or unwilling instructors. After my first day with them, I decided that I would be able to save between five and seven of the ten potential nongraduates. A month later, seven passed their ECL tests.

Living in Saigon and teaching ESL, I often forgot that there was a war going on just miles outside of the city. But at night, I heard the rumblings of the B-52 bombing runs over the surrounding countryside, and I remembered.

Subbing

One morning late in my year, I rolled into school looking forward to a day off. I was on stand-by for a week. We usually got a week of stand-by after teaching two or three consecutive two-week courses. Instead, I found out in the orderly room that I had an assignment to substitute in an Elementary class of enlisted men.

I shrugged as I looked at the class book, and decided on some work to keep the students busy while I read the newspaper and wrote some letters. Some students worked on the assigned exercises while others talked quietly. About halfway through the first hour, I heard a comment and responded without thinking in Vietnamese. Immediately I had all twelve students' attention. A conversation ensued in which we jumped around between my beginner's proficiency in Vietnamese and their beginners' proficiency in English.

They were all quite impressed with my quite unimpressive knowledge of their language. And I realized that that was the key detail. I don't know how many months they had been at the school, but there were no accelerated students in the room. They had either not studied or not been in school to study English before being assigned to mechanics jobs. The fact that when they graduated they'd leave Saigon and go to small bases or jungle outposts limited their abilities and their motivation.

But they were thrilled to hear me speak Vietnamese. They wanted to know how I learned it and what I thought about Vietnam and the war. I became interested in their perspectives because of their interest in mine.

They expressed roughly the same sentiments that their peers and superiors—the officers I'd taught before—had expressed both orally and in their writing. They wanted peace for their country after so many years of war. They wanted a united Vietnam because they all had relatives in the north. Ho Chi Minh was their hero. He was the father of Vietnamese independence. They did not know what democracy was, but they knew what independence was. They also knew that the South Vietnamese government was corrupt.

They understood America's power, but they could not understand America's actions. They talked about what their people needed—houses, schools, and hospitals. And they had great respect for the American standard of living that provided essentials for all of its citizens.

During this discussion, the students smiled and laughed. They told me I was a good teacher. A good person.

And I wondered, What if the United States had sent carpenters and teachers and nurses to Vietnam ten years ago instead of advisors and soldiers? Maybe then we could have won the hearts and minds of the people, and Vietnam would be the ally we sought.

During my last two months, my enjoyment of teaching remained high. In July, I got a brand new class. It was the students' first week, which made it the most difficult class, but I liked it. A month later, I was working with an advanced class, preparing them for the final ECL. I aimed for a two-thirds passing rate.

BJ had a class of enlisted men—mechanics. Six were named Hung. It was one of his favorite classes, but eleven of the twelve students failed their ECL test. When he expressed his disappointment to them, his students explained that they wanted to stay at school as long as possible. Their lives were safer and more comfortable in Tent City than they would be at some base in the middle of central Vietnam.

Hao's Party

One morning at school, Hao, one of my former students, met me before class and invited me to a party in his honor prior to his departure for pilot training. That Friday evening, I went to his home and was greeted by his extended family and friends. Everyone was dressed formally in traditional Vietnamese attire. All of the women were wearing *ao dais*, and all of the men were wearing ornately embroidered jackets with black silk pants.

I soon realized the limits of my Vietnamese. I understood about half of what was said to me, and Hao's family members understood only about one tenth of what I said. Later in the evening, some began to speak English to me. Their English was considerably better than my Vietnamese, but they spoke reluctantly and self-consciously.

It seemed that Americans brandish everything and anything they know, while the Vietnamese conceal what they do not know. We try to show all that we know, and they try not to show what they don't know. I had broadcast my limited Vietnamese boldly into conversations with anyone willing to listen. They had politely struggled to understand me, but withheld their own superior English abilities.

Just as their dress, their dinner, too, was extravagant. Everyone sat on the polished mahogany floor in a large ellipse around an elaborately embroidered tapestry covered with platters of food—sumptuously prepared dishes of beef, pork, chicken, and duck, and numerous rice dishes, and vegetables of all kinds. Some guests sat cross-legged. Some sat upon their heels. Conditioned by a lifetime of sitting on chairs and couches, I was not so limber. My legs ached after a few minutes of sitting cross-legged. I stretched them out diagonally, alternately to my left and then to my right, trying to get comfortable. I was simultaneously struggling with the challenge of being a courteous and respectful guest and yet not recognizing most of the dishes offered to me.

As a spoiled only child, I had grown up on a bland diet of meat and potatoes with an occasional helping of green beans or asparagus, and buttered, salted corn on the cob from the end of July through the beginning of October each summer. I smiled and said "*Cam on*" (Thank you) when offered anything remotely familiar, discarding my apprehension about the flavor of the sauces. But when I had no idea what was being offered, I smiled and said, "*Thoi, cam on*" (No, thank you) and passed the mysterious dishes on.

It was a striking scene. Hao wore his dress uniform, and all of his relatives and friends were present to honor his achievement and express their gratitude to me for being his instructor. I made it through the meal by washing down any too surprising tastes with either tea or beer.

Sergeant Coward

All of the sergeants I knew growing up in Rochester were cartoon characters, some in the newspaper comics and some on TV.

Sarge was always trying to get Beetle Bailey to wake up or get to work.

Sergeant Bilko was always trying to trick his dimwitted officers into providing some benefit to his outfit that it did not deserve.

Sergeant Schultz, the German buffoon, knew "absolutely nothing" about the shenanigans of Colonel Hogan and his POW heroes.

They were all caricatures of soldiers, satires of military life. I'd never known a real sergeant until Technical Sergeant Hecht stepped off of the pages of some unpublished comic book and into my life with his hat brim tilted down and his boots shining like obsidian. His monosyllabic barking during six weeks of basic training challenged my comprehension.

"Get out da bed!" he shouted at me on the second morning.

When he shouted (he never spoke), he wanted to see nothing but "asses and elbows." Hmmm . . . what about the time he summoned us to "Get the hell over here?" Were we supposed to run backwards toward him? Too bad I didn't think to ask him.

After twenty-four years of never knowing a real sergeant and knowing that I'd certainly never be one, I became Sergeant Coward on September 1, 1970. Most airmen didn't get their third stripe until after three of four years, but we, the few, the proud, the Palace Dogs, were rewarded for our critical work teaching English by getting early promotions.

I must admit that I'd often forget and feel good about those three stripes on my sleeves. Just like I had felt about my varsity letters at Penfield. And my A's and B's at Trinity. BJ, Big G, and

I did some real swaggering, carrying all of those stripes around every day. Just like I'd adjusted to living in Saigon, I'd become habituated to being in the Air Force, and I was unconsciously internalizing some of its values.

Orders

As the year's end approached, everyone became obsessed with awaiting orders. When would we know? Where would we be stationed? We had all enlisted in the Air Force for four years, most to avoid combat that would have followed enlisting for two years in the Army. We had all been assigned to DLI and AFLS despite recruiters' promises about OCS, Monterey, and computer training.

Some of my classmates got their orders early. They were headed for Texas, Georgia, Oklahoma, Alabama, and Louisiana. One was going to finish out his service at Wright-Patterson Air Force Base in Dayton, Ohio. That was the closest to New England that I'd heard. I learned that my orders were in, and I could pick them up after school on August 30.

I dashed out of class that afternoon, hopped on my Honda, beat the bus out of the gate, and drove over to MACV Headquarters. Driving down one of the main roads on Tan Son Nhut, I saw an Army pick-up truck coming toward me with its left turn signal on, but I had the right of way, so I kept rolling. At an intersection, the truck turned and nailed me. I was knocked off of my bike and into the air. I was probably only in the air for a second or two, but it seemed like I was floating up there for minutes in astonishment, anger, and pain. When I landed in the road about twenty feet from my bike, I heard the driver say, "Sorry, I didn't even see you."

My left leg was killing me, so badly that I forgot about my orders. An ambulance took me to the hospital, and a doctor explained that there were no broken bones, thanks to my jungle boot. The truck's bumper—steel in those days—pinned my left ankle against the motor of my bike. I was on crutches for a week

and still sore two months later when I reported for duty at Plattsburgh Air Force Base in upstate New York.

I couldn't have gotten any closer to home.

All was set. I would leave Vietnam at 0810 hours on October
21, 1970. I had become so acclimated to teaching English, motor-
cycling around Saigon, studying Vietnamese, playing on the AFLS
basketball team, eating American food at the clubs and Vietnamese food in restaurants, wearing the same clothes every day, and
not really knowing the war that I was confused about my departure. I didn't know whether I was leaving home or going home.

Questions for Discussion

1. How do you think the author's parents felt watching the news about the war on TV every night? How do you think they and other parents of American soldiers in Vietnam felt seeing pictures of injured and dead soldiers every night?

2. Do you think that watching the news made parents feel better or worse about their sons? Why?

3. What details about the author's year in Vietnam were most interesting? Why?

4. What experiences were most significant to the author during his year in Vietnam? Why do you think so?

5. Did his experiences change his perspective on American involvement in Vietnam? Explain.

Part III

Back in the United States (1970–2004)

Homecomings

San Francisco

I sold my motorcycle and packed up my AFLS books, wooden water buffaloes, and Buddhas to be shipped home. I folded my jungle fatigues and refolded the civilian clothes that I had not worn once during the entire year in Saigon, and stuffed them all in my duffel bag. I put on my tan Air Force casual uniform, required traveling attire.

I looked down the aisle of the deserted barracks, recalling chain smoking and discussions about the war and late-night poker games. I walked out onto the small second-floor porch and looked over the rows and rows of barracks all built in the late 1960s to accommodate the increasing numbers of troops. As I looked beyond the rows of barracks, I saw the shops and heard the motorcycles zooming around in the center of Saigon. I missed living there already.

I looped the strap of my duffel bag over my shoulder and walked down the stairs and over to the bus stop to catch a ride to Tan Son Nhut. I waited there in a growing crowd of Army, Navy, Marine, and Air Force survivors—soldiers with only hours remaining in their tours of duty. Many were smiling and laughing. Many had blank expressions on their faces. Most were smoking.

At Tan Son Nhut, the anxious waiting continued. Then our flight was called. We lined up inside the hot and humid terminal. We filed out toward a Braniff 737 gleaming on the tarmac. It was the brightest, cleanest plane any of us had seen in a year. We climbed the shaky stairs and sat quietly as the flight personnel reminded us to fasten our seatbelts. Many snickered when warned about the danger of a bumpy plane ride after surviving a year of jungle combat. Most passengers were subdued. Some whispered in their seats, some fidgeted with the radio and movie controls. Others peered out the windows or stared blankly toward the front of the plane as the pilots revved up the engines, and taxied out onto the runway.

Our plane stopped, and then a roar of the engines pressed us against the backs of our seats. We rocketed down the runway. At the exact moment of liftoff, another roar erupted—survivors cheered leaving Vietnam, where most had seen friends die and faced the ends of their own lives. Few had ever understood it all.

Silence followed the shouts and the applause. Everyone peered out the windows at the peaceful landscape of the Mekong Delta below—meandering rivers and lush green rice paddies and dense jungles. Some soon turned their attention to the movie as if they were returning home at the end of a week's vacation. Others closed their eyes and fell asleep, or stared past the television screens, the stewardesses, and the cockpit, blinking away tears.

Another round of cheers accompanied our landing at Travis Air Force Base just outside of San Francisco, but it was a half-hearted imitation of the roar heard during takeoff. I went in to San Francisco to spend a few days with a friend. Karen Mear was two years older than I and had grown up just across the street on Dale Road. She had married Ted, and they were both really glad to see me. Even though Karen and I had never had a real conversation in twenty years and I had never met Ted before.

I didn't sleep as long as I had expected, and awoke restlessly my first morning back in the United States. I was uncomfortable in this new world that I had once known so well. I purposely stayed in bed until I heard Ted and Karen leave for work. Then I got up, took a long shower, and went out to buy some clothes. I bought a pair of flowered bell-bottom pants and a short-sleeved shirt that I hoped would disguise my name, rank, and serial number. But whenever I went outside, I felt that everyone who looked at me knew that I had been a soldier in Vietnam and hated me. My hair was short, and no one had short hair in California in 1970 except servicemen and their hawkish supporters.

My self-consciousness was intensified because I felt guilty about my participation in what I had begun to realize was a tragic misunderstanding of Vietnam and the Vietnamese by America and the Americans. I spent four days in the city by the bay, sometimes forgetting my year in Vietnam and enjoying the beauty and color and pace of San Francisco life. Other times remembering it vividly and longing to be back in Saigon. I was especially conspicuous at a celebration of Huey Newton's birthday in Golden Gate Park on the weekend. It was both a picnic and a demonstration for civil rights and peace. Half of the people were black Americans with Black Power T-shirts and Afros, and the other half were white Americans with tie-dyed T-shirts and long, flowing hair . . . shoulder length and longer . . . Here, baby . . . There, baby . . . Everywhere, baby, baby . . . Hair!

As out of place as I felt in San Francisco, I felt even more apprehensive about my return to Rochester.

Dale Road

My parents met me at the airport late at night. Mom sputtered her love and relief through her tears, and hugged me tightly. Dad smiled the same feelings, and shook my hand. We walked down the corridor to get my luggage talking about my visit with Karen and Ted, the weather in Rochester, Michigan's upcoming football game against Ohio State, and Mrs. Leonard's appendectomy. Just as if I was coming home from college for Thanksgiving.

When we drove down Dale Road, I saw a "WELCOME HOME RUSS" banner covering the entire side of our house. Friend and neighbor Peter Burrell had fashioned it out of an old bed sheet. Despite my earlier apprehension, I felt more comfortable on Dale Road than I had on Market Street in San Francisco.

Every evening at 6:30, my parents and I watched the news. For as long as I could remember, they always watched the news before dinner. I'm sure they watched it even more closely during the twelve months that I had been in Vietnam. Just like the parents of every other American kid over there.

My parents sat in their respective upholstered chairs, and I sat on the floor close enough to reach the television and change channels from CBS to NBC to ABC, trying to get the most news possible from Vietnam. By November 1970, the United States had reduced its troop strength from 550,000 to less that 300,000, but the fighting was still intense. Each of the three networks allotted almost all of its half hour of evening news to coverage of the war.

New problems were emerging. "Combat refusal" and "fragging" were increasing. "Combat refusal" was the phrase used to describe what in previous wars were only incidents of individual soldiers refusing to obey orders, resulting in court martial and jail sentences or dishonorable discharges. But "combat refusal" in reference to American involvement in Vietnam identified broader mutinies. Often entire platoons refused the orders of their officers to execute a dangerous patrol or initiate a firefight for a patch of jungle or a hill that would only be abandoned at the end of the day. "Fragging" was a slang expression for a new phenomenon in American military history—the killing of officers by their own troops using fragmentation grenades.

Also increasing were reports of small Army or Marine base camps in the jungle being destroyed by sappers. These North Vietnamese or Viet Cong soldiers crawled during the night and rested during the day until they reached the perimeters of the targeted American outposts. Attacking at night, three or four sappers often destroyed stores of munitions and supplies and inflicted heavy casualties on the surprised America troops.

Politicians in Washington were striving to build a democracy in South Vietnam, and military commanders in Vietnam were striving to win the war, but most GIs had a simpler goal. They just wanted to get out alive. Those who had survived four or six or eight months of combat were increasingly reluctant to follow the orders of inexperienced young officers just off the parade grounds of West Point. When new officers issued foolhardy orders, their men often refused to follow them. When the officers persisted in their foolhardiness, they became targets for what were often officially reported as "errantly thrown" grenades. From their own men.

Viewers in their living rooms across the nation had seen and heard reports and films of burning Buddhist monks, American boys dying everywhere in South Vietnam, even accidentally killing each other in friendly fire accidents in the dense jungle. Now viewers were learning that some soldiers were intentionally killing their officers. Attitudes were changing. Even those who had initially supported the war, purportedly being fought to contain communism and build a democracy in South Vietnam, were advocating the end of American involvement.

My initial sense that the U.S. involvement in Vietnam was misguided had been strongly confirmed by my year living there, and I felt compelled to tell everyone everything I had learned. My parents listened patiently. Some of my old high school friends living in Rochester were fascinated, but others didn't want to hear what I had to say. It was the same with my aunts, uncles, and cousins.

Trinity

I decided to take my tale to Connecticut and my old college pals. I drove up to see Bob Gutzman in northwestern Connecticut on the Thursday before Homecoming at Trinity. He was teaching Social Studies and coaching basketball at Housatonic Valley Regional High School. He was also coaching freshman football, and his gridders had a Friday afternoon game. I drove over to the school and parked in the parking lot on the right side of the school that had been dedicated by Eleanor Roosevelt as the first regional high school in Connecticut.

The school sits above its athletic fields that are bordered on the west by the Housatonic River. It was a beautiful early November afternoon with the sun shining just above the hills beyond the river. Bob and his team were down on the field loosening up and waiting for their opponents. I heard a bus pull into the parking lot and swing around to my right. It parked parallel to the field below. Gilbert High School's freshman football players poured off the bus and loped straight down the bank to the field hollering, "Kill! Kill! Kill!"

I could not believe my ears. I had always been a "jock" and

played every game to win, whether it was real or just pickup, but that day I was outraged.

Homecoming at Trinity was a similarly alienating experience. Sophomores who had pledged Sigma Nu my senior year were self-satisfied seniors now. My classmates, who I had seen every day for four years but not once in the last two, were all thrilled to see me. They said so.

"Great to see you, Russ. Hey, weren't you in Vietnam?" asked Bill. "Catch you after the game."

That was it for my college homecoming. I left the fraternity party earlier than I had expected and drove back to Rochester.

After a week of getting reacclimated to living in a house with comfortable furniture and a refrigerator full of food, I threw some books and clothes into the 1966 Oldsmobile Cutlass that my Dad had bought for me and drove up to Plattsburgh. I had a room on the second floor of the 380th Wing Headquarters Squadron barracks, and I worked on the first floor in the Orderly Room. I was the squadron's Supervisor of OJT (On-the-Job Training) and GMT (General Military Training).

Plattsburgh Air Force Base

My work was mostly paperwork, with some driving around the base to different job sites, too. I made friends with guys who had served in Vietnam and guys who played basketball. When we weren't in the gym, we were playing poker or shooting pool or listening to music and drinking beer. Just like Hemingway's immortalized "lost generation" of young men who survived World War I, we felt alone and alienated, unable to communicate with our peers who had only watched the war on TV or read the headlines from Vietnam in the newspapers.

About a month after my return, the trial of Lieutenant William Calley for his actions at My Lai began. It dominated the news for months. Some Americans were horrified by his actions, and demanded his punishment. Others felt that as unfortunate as the My Lai incident was, it was just what happened in war. Still, others felt that Calley was being made a scapegoat for the commanders who bore the real responsibility for free fire zones, search and destroy missions, and the resulting body-count mania.

I knew that American boys were getting killed and maimed every day. And they were killing innocent Vietnamese every day. I could not see anyone in America benefiting from these actions. I did not know why more Americans did not want to end the war.

While home for Christmas in 1970, everyone in the Dale Road neighborhood was urging me to get in touch with Jim Rattigan because "He was in Vietnam, too." He was the kid I had admired growing up, but I felt that we had gone in quite different directions from our days playing World War II games and later baseball in Corbett's Glen.

One late afternoon during the week between Christmas and New Year's, I heard a knock at the back door of my parents' house and was surprised to see Jim and his wife Pat standing on our porch. I invited them in and Jim and I chatted all around our experiences in Vietnam. I talked about teaching English in Saigon, and Jim talked about the country and the cities and the weather and the food—everything except combat. Neither of us wanted to talk about that. It was almost dinner time, so we both repeated how glad we were to see each other and promised to keep in touch when we were back in Rochester at the same times. Jim and Pat walked the quarter mile back to his parents' house and I never saw him again.

After the holidays, I returned to Plattsburgh, and Jim moved on to assignments at the Pentagon, Quantico, and Paris Island, and was promoted to Major. He got sick and was eventually diagnosed with leukemia, but a complete bone marrow transplant at the Fred Hutchinson Hospital in Seattle was not covered by his military benefits because it could not be proven that his illness was caused by his exposure to Agent Orange. Funds were raised to help Jim by his Marine buddies and his Nichols College and Penfield High classmates. He recovered temporarily from his bone marrow transplant, but died two years later.

In the spring of 1971, John Kerry and a half dozen fellow Vietnam veterans formed Vietnam Veterans Against the War (VVAW). "How could this group not capture the nation's attention and get its message across?" I wondered. They demonstrated in Washington for five days in April 1971, calling their actions "a limited incursion into the country of Congress." Physically and psychologically scarred by their experiences in Vietnam, veterans spoke against the war and hurled their medals onto the steps of the Capitol. "Yes!" I thought, blinking away tears while watching television in Plattsburgh.

Soon the impact of the VVAW was clear. The FBI declared the group the second greatest threat to national security. Kerry's career in politics continued. He served in Congress as a Senator from Massachusetts, and in 2003 campaigned for the Democratic presidential nomination. By the spring of 2004, Kerry was acknowledged as the Democrat who would receive his party's nomination and oppose President George W. Bush in the November election.

In June 1971, U.S. Department of Defense employee Daniel Ellsberg leaked to *New York Times* correspondent Neil Sheehan and later *Washington Post* correspondent Ben Bagdikian copies of The Pentagon Papers, a 7,000-page review of America's thirty-year involvement in Indochina that documented the discrepancies between what the American political and military leaders knew and what they had been telling the American people. The Papers presented the truth behind the lies that had been disseminated for nearly a decade. The *Times* and the *Post* were ordered not to print the Papers, but the Supreme Court ruled in favor of freedom of the press and against the power of the President. But Ellsberg joined VVAW at the top of the FBI's most dangerous list.

In an interview with Daryl Lindsey of Salon.com on April 28, 2000, Ellsberg commented that he wished he had acted earlier than he had. "My only regret," he said, "is that I didn't do it a number of years earlier, when they might have had a much more powerful effect in averting the war or ending it. If I had released the papers in '64 or '65 when I was in the Pentagon, there might not have been any war. And we might have averted 58,000 American dead and millions of Vietnamese [deaths]. That's a heavy responsibility, but, unfortunately, I didn't imagine doing it at that time."

In the aftermath of the release of the Pentagon Papers, the controversy continued. In 1972, napalm, Watergate, and South Dakota Senator George McGovern captured everyone's attention.

On June 8, 1972, one of the thousands of napalm sprayings used to destroy the jungle sanctuary of the NVN regulars and the VC irregulars went awry. On that afternoon, napalm was sprayed over the village of Trang Bang, twenty-five miles from Saigon. Associated Press (AP) photojournalist Nick Ut snapped a picture of five Vietnamese children running out of the village screaming and crying. In the center was a naked nine-year-old girl named Kim Phuc. Running down the center of a wet road, she was holding her arms away from her body and her face was contorted in agony. "My clothes were burned right off," she commented years later in the book that chronicled her life, *The Girl in the Picture* by Denise Chong.

Later, historian David Halberstam, speaking in "Unsung He-

Nine-year-old Kim Phuc, *center*, runs down Route 1 near Trang Bang after an aerial napalm attack on suspected Viet Cong hiding places on June 8, 1972. A South Vietnamese plane accidentally dropped its flaming napalm on South Vietnamese troops and civilians. © AP/Wide World Photos.

roes" on the History Channel, described the photo as "The touchstone picture of the Vietnam War." Nick Ut had been walking toward Trang Bang just as Kim and other villagers were running away. He snapped the picture and then took Kim to the nearest hospital. "He saved my life," Kim says.

Initial treatment revealed that Kim was so severely burned that she had to be immediately transferred to the elite Barsky burn clinic in Saigon. For nearly a year, her survival was uncertain. Eventually she was able to lead a somewhat normal life, but then became the political property of the Vietnamese government. In 1992, she defected in Newfoundland during a stop on a flight from Moscow to Cuba. She subsequently became a Canadian citizen.

In 1999, addressing a gathering of photographers in upstate

New York, reflecting on the significance of her universally recognized picture, Kim said, "Sometimes I think of that little girl screaming, running up the road, as not being a symbol of war, but a symbol of a cry for peace."

Little more than a week after the picture of Kim Phuc had circled the world, news of Watergate was on the front page of every newspaper. On June 17, 1972, a break-in at the national headquarters of the Democratic Party in the Watergate complex in Washington, D.C., was interrupted. First rumors and eventually facts linked the break-in to President Nixon and the Republican Party.

That fall, Nixon's bid for re-election was being challenged by Democratic nominee George McGovern, who was running on a simple campaign platform—withdraw American troops from Vietnam. Nixon boasted, "The United States will not leave Vietnam with its tail between its legs."

McGovern's call for immediate withdrawal was unpopular. To do so would be to acknowledge a mistake. A misunderstanding of international politics. And a wasting of the lives of some 50,000 American boys.

But I was excited on Election Day in November of 1972. I hoped that Americans would do the right thing and elect McGovern. I drove to the polling place in Treadwell Mills, just outside of Plattsburgh, eager to cast my vote for the truth and what was morally right. It was a small rectangular VFW building in the middle of an unspectacular park. There were a half dozen picnic tables, a small playground, two tennis courts, and a basketball court.

All of the hope that had grown within me during the campaign was dispelled when I walked into the VFW that night. I knew that the tally from Treadwell Mills was going to be something like Nixon 278–McGovern 1. And that was the way the whole country went. Massachusetts was the only state that McGovern won. Nixon won the Election of 1972 in a landslide.

Today, I am struck by the bleak irony of Johnson's record landslide victory in the election of 1964 followed two elections (eight years) later by a new record landslide in favor of the opposite party, even though virtually nothing had changed in the United

States or regarding U.S. involvement in Vietnam. The Republic of South Vietnam was still a fiction authored and funded by American politicians, and Americans were increasingly polarized about the whole story.

By April 1973, Nixon had withdrawn all American troops from Vietnam. Just as McGovern had promised. That withdrawal was made possible by the Paris Accords, agreements among representatives of North Vietnam, South Vietnam, and the United States. Secretary of State Kissinger was the lead American negotiator, and Le Duc Tho led the North Vietnamese contingent. North Vietnam agreed to return all American POWs. South Vietnam agreed to return all North Vietnamese POWs. America agreed to withdraw all of its troops from South Vietnam.

South Vietnam strongly opposed allowing North Vietnamese troops to remain in the South, but acceded to American pressure on the basis of unofficial promises of continuing America support in equipment and dollars.

Kissinger and Tho were named co-winners of the Nobel Peace Prize. Kissinger was present in Stockholm to receive his award, but Tho did not attend the ceremonies, explaining that for his people the war was not over. South Vietnamese President Nguyen Van Thieu concurred. While Americans were celebrating the end of the Vietnam War, Thieu announced the beginning of the Third Indochina War.

As the last American troops were leaving Tan Son Nhut in the spring of 1973, I was packing boxes and suitcases in a trailer home outside of Plattsburgh, finishing my four years in the USAF. By sheer coincidence I had a place to go, too.

I had been accepted into a master's program in the Graduate School of Education and Human Development at the University of Rochester. I had decided that I wanted to teach high school English.

University of Rochester

I lived with my parents on Dale Road during the summer of 1973 until moving into graduate housing at the University of Rochester to begin what I expected to be a two-year stay to get my master's degree. But grad school in education turned out to be much more interesting than I had been led to believe. My years in the Air Force, especially the year in Vietnam, had changed me in ways that I gradually began to recognize. In simple terms, I had gained an interest in the lives of others. I was no longer just a self-centered kid from a loving middle-class family who took his good fortune for granted.

Throughout that summer, my parents and I gathered in the living room every evening to watch the news. Vietnam no longer dominated the news as it had when American boys were fighting and dying there, but it was still getting significant coverage each evening.

When I moved over to the University of Rochester, I continued to catch either the 6:30 or 11:00 news every day. For a year and a half, there was continuous heavy combat between the ARVN and NVN forces, but no significant changes in the overall situation. In 1974, 31,000 ARVN soldiers were killed. But America's attention was focused on Washington, D.C. The grand jury investigation following the interrupted break-in at Watergate culminated in the House Judiciary Committee approving three articles of impeachment, charging President Nixon with misusing his power in order to violate the constitutional rights of U.S. citizens, obstructing justice in the Watergate affair, and defying Judiciary Committee subpoenas. Nixon resigned on August 9, 1974, and Gerald Ford was sworn in as the 38th president of the United States.

In the first week of March 1975, everyone's attention shifted back to Vietnam as the North Vietnamese tanks crossed the DMZ and rolled southward down the Ho Chi Minh Trail. A decade earlier it had taken DRV soldiers three to six months to walk the many paths through the dense jungle in the Truong Son mountains on the Vietnam–Laos border to make the journey south to support their NLF comrades. By 1975, the Trail had been paved. Reading about the Trail while writing this narrative, I experienced the persistence of my own cultural bias. I had been writing about the Ho Chi Minh Trail as if that was the name of that region and not recognizing the obvious fact that this name was given by American commanders to the route taken by the enemy soldiers. To the Vietnamese, it was the Truong Son Trail, named logically after the mountainous route it followed. This final push to eradicate the South Vietnamese regime and reunify Vietnam was called the Ho Chi Minh Campaign. DRV leaders anticipated that it would require a two-year effort. It lasted fifty-five days.

DRV troops took Ban Me Thuot in the Central Highlands. Then Da Nang. Then Hue. Then Xuan Loc on April 12. ARVN troops challenged this march as it moved to threaten Saigon. President Thieu's repeated pleas for U.S. aid were to no avail with Nixon out of office. President Ford announced that "America has a moral responsibility to Vietnam," but he took no action. Thieu resigned after the fall of Xuan Loc, and was taken to Taipei. He eventually moved on to England and then to Foxboro, Massachusetts, where he died on September 29, 2001.

A desperate evacuation of South Vietnamese politicians and military leaders closely associated with the United States occurred at the same time that the DRV tanks rolled into Saigon. In a mere formality, Thieu's temporary replacement, Duoung Van Minh, surrendered to Colonel Bui Tin, who proclaimed, "The war has ended today, and all Vietnamese are victors. Only the American imperialists are the vanquished." Vietnam was reunified, an independent nation thirty years after Ho Chi Minh had so proclaimed it, and twenty years after it had been partitioned by the superpowers at Geneva.

In a way, one phase of my life had ended. I left Vietnam for grad school. Friends had warned me that grad school in education would be boring, but my work at Rochester was just the opposite. I was able to take English and sociology and anthropology and law courses, and in those courses I was able to connect my five years of post-college experiences to the theoretical issues being addressed by texts, articles, and class discussions. I wrote a paper on education in Vietnam for my International Education course, and I wrote a paper on military training for my Sociology of Education course. And I was given the freedom to create my own reading list for an independent study in curriculum course.

My advisor, Bill Pinar, was my age and a leader of a radical group of curricular theorists referred to as the "Reconceptualists." They wanted to change students' experience of schooling, and I wanted to educate students differently than I had been schooled.

To support myself, I worked about thirty hours a week at a local moving company. I had a New York State War Service scholarship and monthly G.I. Bill checks, but they fell far short of their originally legislated goal. Passed after World War I, the G.I. Bill was designed to enable discharged veterans to attend college. It was supposed to pay for tuition, room, and board, and it did for a decade, perhaps. But it had never been adjusted for inflation.

I immersed myself in my grad work, but in 1974 a film entitled *Hearts and Minds* caught my attention. I still cared deeply about how the war was perceived and presented to Americans. Peter Davis's documentary showed viewers how American actions in Vietnam diverged from the words of the politicians. One scene showed a football coach whipping his team into a halftime frenzy in their locker room and then flashed to a battlefield in Vietnam. Sitting in the theater, I remembered my visit to Connecticut in November 1970 and the freshman football team charging down the hill yelling, "Kill!"

Later, the movie presented a close-up of General Westmoreland, Commander in Chief of the American forces in Vietnam, explaining that "The Vietnamese don't put the same value on human life that we do." Again the film shifted scenes immediately. To a Vietnamese woman sobbing uncontrollably at her husband's graveside. *Hearts and Minds* won the Oscar for Best Documentary in 1974.

I told everyone I knew to see the film. Few did.

But most bought tickets to *The Deer Hunter*, starring Robert De Niro. So did I. Ambivalently. I was simultaneously apprehensive and curious to see how Hollywood would deliver Vietnam to the American public for profit. Following a panoramic and pictur- esque tour of Clairton, Pennsylvania, a steel mill town that young De Niro's character ruled by charisma, but not financial or polit- ical clout, viewers follow him to Vietnam where he is captured by the communists.

The "bad guys" in tattered khakis forced De Niro and, implic- itly, all other American POWs to play Russian Roulette—place a single bullet in a chamber of a revolver, spin the cylinder, place the barrel of the gun at your temple, and pull the trigger. Click . . . the hammer strikes an empty chamber. Or bang . . . you're dead. Hollywood presented it well. So well that the audience gasped each time. And when De Niro turned the tables on his Vietnamese captors, killed one, and escaped, the audience erupted with cheers. Many viewers actually bolted up out of their seats, clapping and cheering wildly.

Thousands of Americans, whose only knowledge of Vietnam had come via television or the movies, walked out of movie the- aters cursing the horrible Vietnamese who had made American prisoners play such a horrific game. But they felt good knowing that De Niro had finally won.

Certainly prisoners are abused on all sides in any war. And I know that horrors were committed by both Vietnamese and Americans when dealing with captured enemy soldiers, but Rus- sian Roulette was not among them. *The Deer Hunter*'s director, Michael Cimino, had intended Russian Roulette to be a metaphor for the American soldiers' universal experience of being in combat in Vietnam. Many died. Many more survived. But even the sur- vivors were scarred forever by the experience of awakening every day and never knowing if they would live to sleep another night.

Of course, most viewers did not perceive Cimino's perfect meta- phor. I missed it, too. They thought that this central plot detail was historical fact. But I was skeptical. And when my research taught me about the central metaphor, I added an objective to my future lesson plans: Learners will understand that *The Deer Hunter* presents a metaphor for combat, not the literal truth about treatment of American POWs during the Vietnam War.

Following all of the post-Watergate revelations about Republican misdeeds during the Nixon administration, it was no surprise that Jimmy Carter defeated Gerald Ford in the election of 1976. What did surprise people was President Carter's bold step the day after his inauguration. On January 21, 1977, he pardoned all Vietnam-era draft evaders. His decision revived feelings that still polarized Americans. Many people commended Carter's pardon as a great step toward reconciliation, and others condemned it as a dishonor to all the American boys who had served in Vietnam.

In May 1979, I graduated from the University of Rochester with a doctorate in Curriculum and Instruction, but I decided that I would rather teach English and coach basketball at a high school than teach Education at a university.

Housatonic Valley Regional High School

Bob Gutzman called to tell me that there was an English job open at Housatonic Valley Regional High School, and he was also looking for an assistant basketball coach. I made it through four interviews for the teaching job, and Bob welcomed me as his JV coach without another one. At the time, I thought I was prepared to coach but not teach, but by the end of the year, it was obvious that I had had it absolutely backwards.

Also at the end of that year, on June 30, 1980, to be exact, I tried once again to achieve a goal that I had pursued often a decade earlier while teaching in Vietnam, and occasionally during grad school. I stopped smoking. During that summer, I often remembered BJ and me trying to run the tar and nicotine out of our bodies and our psyches. And never feeling bad enough not to light up another Marlboro right after a shower.

I stopped for four years. I wasn't smoking, but I still wanted to smoke. This was also a time when I sort of lost touch with Vietnam. I met only two people in northwestern Connecticut who had any connection to Vietnam: A guy with whom I played basketball who had been in combat and did not want to talk about it, and Bob's neighbors Ed and Stephanie Krukowski, whose son had been killed in Vietnam on June 10, 1965. They didn't mention it when we met, but Bob told me later.

In the early 1980s, a struggling third-world communist nation did not merit much news coverage by the American media. All contacts had been formally broken since the end of the war, and the United States had implemented an embargo blocking all trade with Vietnam. There were no diplomatic relations and no travel permitted for Vietnamese or Americans wanting to go either way.

The Vietnam Veterans Memorial

Then chance brought me back to Vietnam. In the fall of 1985, I was recruited by my school's principal to attend the annual National Council of Teachers of English (NCTE) conference in Washington, D.C. Caught up in the daily scramble of teaching and coaching, it did not occur to me that I'd have a chance to visit the Vietnam Veterans Memorial until I was actually on the plane for D.C.

For years, the treatment of Vietnam veterans had been lamented by them and their supporters. In April 1979, a group of Vietnam veterans incorporated the nonprofit Vietnam Veterans Memorial Fund (VVMF). As indicated by its name, the memorial was intended to honor those who had served, not the war itself. Fourteen months later, President Carter signed the law to provide a site for the memorial in Constitution Gardens near the Lincoln Memorial.

On May 1, 1981, the design of Maya Ying Lin, an undergraduate student at Yale, was announced as the winning submission. Over a thousand designs had been submitted meeting the criteria of being reflective and contemplative, harmonious with the surroundings, including the names of all who had died or were still missing, and making no political statement about the war. Lin's design featured black granite slabs that were shipped from Bangalore, India, to Barre, Vermont, for cutting and finishing.

Construction began in March 1982, and the Memorial was dedicated on Veterans' Day in November 1982. It was paid for by 9 million dollars provided by private donations from corporations, foundations, unions, veterans' organizations, civic organizations, and over a quarter of a million individual American citizens. Names of the dead and missing are in chronological order according to the date of the casualty, and in alphabetical order for each day. The controversy swirling around the memorial and its design did not disappear even after its completion, however. Subsequently, a traditional statue of three soldiers and a flag were added just off to the west side of the Memorial.

Small lights in the ground illuminate the wall of the Vietnam Memorial in Washington, D.C. © AP/Wide World Photos.

Just as there had been a half dozen years of controversy between the conception and completion of the Memorial, there had been a persistent conflict within my own mind about ever visiting it. Both celebratory attitudes toward the war and disdainful attitudes toward those who served and died in Vietnam made me uncomfortable.

I couldn't decide whether I wanted to see it or not. After dinner one evening at the conference, I called up my friend Chris Pyron, who was living in the area, and we arranged to meet on the Constitution Avenue side of the Mall at 9:00. We had met at Plattsburgh AFB following my year in Saigon and his stint in Da Nang. He was nineteen from California. I was twenty-five and from New York, but our experience in Vietnam enabled us to communicate across some of our other barriers.

Our rendezvous was as scheduled, and we proceeded to walk into the Mall, not sure of the memorial's location.

We almost fell into it. Its polished black granite walls had been placed below ground level. The path in front of the Memorial is actually a path below street level.

We walked carefully around the perimeter until we came to the entrance, just a path really, inclined slightly to lead visitors down into the Memorial. I walked a few steps down the inclined path and paused. I just reached out my left hand to touch this impassive memorial to over 58,000 lives ended too soon. I stepped back and read the name in the reflected street lights.

EDWARD E. KRUKOWSKI

I was stunned by the coincidence of touching the name of the son of the couple I had met in Connecticut. The only other name that I would have known was that of my fraternity brother, Buddy Kupka.

Research for this narrative has added details to my personal experience. According to the VVMF Web site, Edward Eugene Krukowski was born in Syracuse, New York, on November 6, 1940. He was "killed in action June 10, 1965, by ground casualty multiple fragmentation wounds hostile . . . while missing in province or military region unknown in South Vietnam . . . body was recovered."

Since the VVMF Web site offers links to other sites, I checked for information about other soldiers who died on June 10, 1965. I found that in addition to Edward, nine other Army soldiers were reported "killed in action while missing in province or military region unknown . . . bodies recovered." Three other Army infantrymen are still MIA from that day. I wonder how that many men could have been killed and had their bodies recovered when no one knew where they were . . . or how no one could know where that many soldiers were.

And I began to think about the timeline and troop levels of the war. It was supposedly not until the spring of 1965 that combat soldiers had been sent to Vietnam, and the first ones were all Marines. So Edward must have been one of the first Army officers sent to fight in Vietnam, and he must have died so soon after getting there, I thought. But when I did some more searching, I discovered that his tour of duty in Vietnam had begun on September 26, 1964. Either he had been sent there as an advisor and later been assigned to combat, or the reported timeline and troop level information was not correct.

I was also interested in the remembrances posted on the site for Edward E. Krukowski. On November 11, 1998, his cousin Dennis Krukowski wrote, "Peace be with you, Edward."

On January 24, 1999, biographical researcher Clay Marston wrote, "Captain Edward Eugene Krukowski was a distinguished graduate of the United Sates Military Academy at West Point in the Class of 1962 who was serving as an infantry line officer on the date of his untimely death . . . and was posthumously awarded the Purple Heart Medal."

On February 21, 2001, Major Richard J. Sloma wrote, "In memory of a comrade a generation apart . . . I was almost one year old when you were killed. Though I never knew you, I have always felt a connection to you. We were from the same neighborhood, the same parish and attended the same school. I used to buy candy from your parents' store. I used to play in Pulaski Park and read your name on the obelisk that stood in front of the church in which you, too, probably served as an altar boy. Like you, I was one of the few persons from our neighborhood who became a commissioned officer in the Army. During my eighteen years in the military . . . I have been entrusted with the lives of young men and women in uniform. As I reflected on my responsibilities, I would remember the sacrifice that you made and the loss your family suffered. In that way, I have carried the memory of your sacrifice within me, I know that the inspiration that you have given me throughout my service has made a difference. I salute you."

On November 7, 2001, Marge Kohanski, who defined her relationship as "We grew up together," wrote, "In remembrance of a friend and next door neighbor."

ANTHONY E. KUPKA

I did not find Buddy's name that night at the Memorial, but I've since learned that it is etched on the 95th line of Panel 27 West. Edward Krukowski had been one of the first to fall in combat. Buddy Kupka had been one of the many to fall in the middle of the hostilities. He died on April 16, 1969, of "multiple fragmentation wounds hostile" on Hill 146 just outside the village of An Hoa in the province of Quang Nam. Exactly one month after his arrival in Vietnam, and three days after the birth of his daughter. He never received the news. He was a platoon leader out on a three-week reconnaissance patrol in the dense jungle.

On March 28, 2000, Vietnam veteran Edward Sprague who served under Buddy wrote, "Lt. Kupka was one of the finest officers I met while serving in the Marine Corps. There is not a day that goes by that I do not think about what happened April 16, 1969."

On April 16, 2002, self-identified "grateful American" Richard Cumberland wrote, "Anthony is not forgotten. He has sacrificed his young life and his entire future so that we can embrace the freedom that is America. God bless you, Anthony."

Childhood friend Richard Besley has written, "I think of you every day of my life. The good times we spent together . . . playing ball together and just being friends . . . never thought we would both go off to war and only one return."

Dan Kellum was Buddy's platoonmate back in Quantico. He wrote on May 1, 2002, "Tony and I were in the same platoon at the Basic School at Quantico from September 1968 through February of 1969. . . . He and his wife were expecting their first child and he lamented the fact that he might be in Vietnam at the time of the child's birth. I told him that I wished I could trade places with him as I was to be sent to Camp Lejeune, NC. He was in-country one month when someone on his 1rst Recon Battalion patrol (Team Nail Brush) in the boonies stepped on a booby trap killing Tony and two other Marines and injuring six others on April 16. He was the first of 3-69 [the platoon that arrived in Vietnam in March, 1969] to die. His team had been inserted April 2 in the bush and was scheduled for a 21-day patrol. I heard the news of his baby girl's birth April 13 never reached him. That has always bothered me. I miss him. Semper Fi."

Marine veteran Frank Porpotage, who served with Buddy in Vietnam, has posted a picture of his smiling "best friend," and wrote lamenting, ". . . the very short time we were together. Semper Fi."

In 1981, the Landon School in Bethesda, Maryland, established the Anthony Edward Kupka '64 Distinguished Alumnus Award. It is the highest award bestowed on alumni of Landon, honoring Buddy in the following words, "During his years at Landon, Buddy exemplified all the qualities of citizenship, integrity and diligence Landon has always sought to instill in its students."

There were over 58,000 names etched into the granite slabs of the Vietnam Veterans Memorial, casualties of America's longest and only undeclared war. At its end, there were another approximately 70,000 young American men missing from their hometowns and family dinner tables. They were draft evaders and deserters who went to live in Canada.

Chris and I continued our walk silently back up to street level. Our conversation was minimal for another half hour while we sipped beers at the bar in the Hyatt.

At Housatonic, I was often invited to speak to American History students about Vietnam. I told them that I was just like them. Oblivious. Living happily in high school in America. And then I got dropped off over there and learned a few things. I emphasized the fear of communism, the probability of about 50,000 out of 2,000,000 Americans dying in the jungles even if there wasn't a war, my Vietnamese students' reverence for Ho Chi Minh, and the fact that in 1954 there was not a single factory in the entire country of Vietnam manufacturing any type of gun. So if the Americans hadn't given every ARVN (South Vietnamese) soldier an M-16 and the Russians and Chinese hadn't given every PAVN (North Vietnamese) soldier an AK-47, there might have been a lot of bruised and sore and maybe even some lacerated enemies, but not hundreds of thousands of parents without their children and children without their parents.

Requiem

I don't remember how I learned about *Requiem*, an exhibition of photographs of 135 photographers who had either been killed or were missing in action in Vietnam.

On a beautiful day in April 1995, I took the train to Grand Central Station in New York City. Out of the darkness, I strolled into the brilliant sunshine illuminating spots and casting shadows in the canyons of the city. Walking down the sidewalk, I wondered about how I'd react. How gruesome would the pictures be? Would they all be of the agony of Americans or would they all be of the agony of Vietnamese? Would there be more shots of soldiers or noncombatants . . . "collateral damage?"

I slowed down unintentionally, maybe even obliviously. As I approached the building where the exhibition was being held, I looked through the windows and saw an enlarged photo of the back of an old SLR. It could have been a Pentax or a Cannon, or even a slightly older model of the Minolta that I was carrying with me. But on the right side of the back of the camera there was an exit wound. If it was being used when it was shot, then its owner had the right side of his head blown away. If it was just hanging from his neck, depending on which way it was swinging, then he had died of a chest wound.

I had toughened myself up in preparation for the horrors of human suffering captured on film, but this photo of a dead camera ambushed me. My walk slowed. My heart was pounding harder and harder. I could not blink away the tears. I inhaled deeply, trying to regain my composure, slowed, and walked into the building.

An enlarged picture of the SLR, the size of a movie screen, loomed above the stairway. I could have crawled through the bullet hole. During a quick tour of the first floor, I saw pictures that I recognized from my years in high school and college, reading *Life* each week as if Vietnam was fiction and not real stories and photos of real people living and dying on the other side of the world.

These photographs were almost familiar and had little impact. I recovered from the ambush on the sidewalk.

I walked downstairs, and midway in my tour of the pictures of mud and water and jungles and corpses and threatening American soldiers and cowering Vietnamese, I discovered a story. It was told in four picture-chapters.

In the first, a young American officer strides across a runway carrying an M-60 machine gun in each hand. He wears brand new camouflaged jungle fatigues, and his hat is cocked slightly back and to his right. Even stopped by the camera shutter, his stride is assured. He smiles. A warrior looking forward to battle.

In the second, he grimaces as he fires an M-60 out of the right side of a helicopter. He wears headphones to protect his ears from the sound of his weapon and a small microphone to enable him to communicate with the pilot.

In the third, he screams toward the back of the chopper for help for the injured soldier lying at his feet, bleeding from wounds in his arm, chest, and leg.

In the final picture-chapter, the young officer sits alone in a supply shack on a crate. Leaning on a second level of boxes, he sobs, his head on his right forearm and his left hand over the left side of his face.

I blinked away tears. I had been angered by his eagerness for combat, but was saddened for him now that he had seen fear and death. It struck me that this simple series of photos—four black-and white-images of a single soldier in a single firefight—told all of the stories of all of the American soldiers and all of the men who had sent them to Vietnam. They all began confident in their cause and eventual victory. They all winced in combat. They all screamed at the unfolding horror. And they all sobbed at the end.

Eventually, the effect of *Requiem* dissipated. There were too many images of too much human suffering. Especially on a sunny Saturday afternoon in New York City. I left the exhibit and walked over to the new Nike store on 57th Street. I entered without hesitating. But as I walked from crowded floor to floor, from sport to sport, from tennis to basketball to running, I was still staring at the camera that had been killed in action, trying to make sense out of my year in Vietnam more than twenty years earlier and my country's years there. And trying to understand why *Requiem* was nearly empty while the Nike store was so mobbed that it was hard to walk around.

A Visit to Vietnam

In April 2001, I returned to Vietnam. I flew American Airlines from New York to Vancouver and Cathay Pacific from Vancouver to Hong Kong. Then I boarded an Air Vietnam plane for Ho Chi Minh City, the renamed Saigon.

I landed at Tan Son Nhut. As the airplane taxied to the terminal, I saw abandoned hangars, rusted trucks, and planes left by the departing U.S. soldiers twenty-eight years earlier. What had been the busiest air base in the world for a decade was now merely a single glistening new terminal surrounded by hundreds of acres of a ghost base.

On the ride into the center of town, I noticed an increase in the quantity and the quality of the traffic. There were even more motorcycles, cars, and trucks than there had been thirty-one years earlier, and the ones on the road were newer, shinier, and slicker. Smoke-belching relics had been replaced by Hondas, Toyotas, and Mitsubishis.

I stayed at the Continental, a hotel that I had only gazed at in awe in 1970, for 40 dollars a day. And breakfast was included— a lavish combination Western and Eastern buffet.

The exchange rate had increased nearly a thousand fold. For a dollar in 1970, I received 118 dong. For a dollar in 2001, I received 15,000 dong. So, exchanging a hundred dollars gave me a million and a half Vietnamese dong. Vietnam runs on cash more than plastic, so I was walking around with a pocketful of 500- and 1,000-dong bills.

I learned that the U.S. Embassy had been leveled, and the new embassy was in Hanoi. It had been opened by Douglas Peterson, a former POW appointed as the first ambassador to the Socialist Republic of Vietnam by President Clinton, who had reestablished diplomatic relations in 1995.

The Continental Hotel in the center of Ho Chi Minh City. Graham Greene wrote *The Quiet American* here, and many American journalists filed reports here during the war.

In the 1980s, I had learned of the CIA's role in the assassination of Diem when watching the PBS series on Vietnam War. In Saigon in 2001, I met a former South Vietnamese officer who commented, "It is said that he wanted to collaborate with the North."

I took a tour to the ancient city of Hoi An, the principal city of Da Nang just south of the DMZ, and the imperial capital of Hue. My guide had grown up in Hanoi and was the son of a retired North Vietnamese General. His father had been one of the original Viet Minh. He had spent most of his life as a soldier in southern Vietnam. He had fought against the Japanese, the French, the Americans, and the Chinese. He explained that about nine months after each of his father's visits to Hanoi, he had gained a brother or a sister. He also noted with pride that Vietnam was the only nation in the world to have defeated three members of the United Nations Security Council—China, France, and the United States—in war.

In Hue, I visited the Ho Chi Minh Museum, one of nearly two hundred throughout the country honoring the man who first

Statue of Ho Chi Minh in the Ho Chi Minh Museum in Hue.

dreamed of, then spoke of, and eventually proclaimed the independence of Vietnam. It was a beautiful modern building, brighter than any of the museums I later visited in Ho Chi Minh City.

Back in Ho Chi Minh City after my tour of central Vietnam, I visited the tunnels of Cu Chi, now enlarged and open to the public as one of the numerous memorials located across the country in every city, town, village, and hamlet "To remember forever" the Vietnamese soldiers who sacrificed their lives in the American War, as it is referred to in Vietnam. There are over 58,000 names on the Cu Chi Memorial, approximately the same number of names on the Vietnam Veterans Memorial in Washington. If America had lost the same proportion of its male population that Vietnam had, there would be over twelve million names on the polished black granite slabs set into the ground on the Mall in Washington.

When I had been living in Saigon, I heard the rumblings of the B-52 bombings every evening in the distance. Cu Chi was one of the areas most heavily hit. But the intensive bombing did not eliminate the Viet Cong. They were living underground. At the time, U.S. soldiers realized that the VC were using a tunnel system for refuge, but they had no idea how extensive the system was. They had underground living quarters, hospitals, mess halls, and schools. Some Viet Cong lived underground for years.

"All memorials are the same," I thought. Gettysburg, Normandy, Stalingrad, and Cu Chi. All honor the individuals who have sacrificed their lives for their countries. It's simple. These men are dead, and their surviving parents and wives and children and friends wish that they were still alive.

All visitors to Cu Chi are shown a film prior to entering the area of the tunnels. It is in black and white and has a glaring bias against the Americans who came like "a batch of crazy devils . . . to kill this small piece of country thousands of miles from their homes." It concludes by honoring the "Vietnamese peasants who became heroes with a rifle in one hand and a plow in the other. . . . Every person was a soldier."

The city's newest museum was less harshly anti-American. I learned that its name has been changed twice. It opened a mere five months after the North Vietnamese tanks rolled into Saigon. From September 1974 until 1990, the museum was named "The Exhibition House about the American and former Saigon Government's War Crimes." In late 1990, the name was changed to "The Exhibition House about the Aggressors' War Crimes." On July 4, 1995, exactly one week before the formal restoration of diplomatic relations between the United States and Vietnam, the name was changed to "The War Remnants Museum." Its symbol is a white dove in the foreground covering the middle third of three vertical bombs pointing down in the background, visible in black above and in red below the dove.

A walk through the exhibits moves from horror to hope. First, images of war are presented. These are followed by pictures of the effects of Agent Orange—adults with cancerous growths on their bodies and young children with hideously deformed or missing limbs. I asked a guide if visiting American veterans ever became angry or hostile when viewing the exhibitions. She softly explained, "Some U.S. veterans when they visit the museum they cry. Many offer their medals to this museum saying, 'I'm sorry. We were wrong.' "

An entire room is filled with posters and quotations from all

Author in a conference room at the War Remnants Museum.

over the world expressing opposition to the American involvement in Vietnam. Featured prominently here are pictures and
words of Martin Luther King and Robert McNamara. King's 1969
entreaty was, "Come home Americans. Come home from your
dark country of racism, from your tragic, reckless adventure in
Vietnam." McNamara's words from *In Retrospect* are displayed
boldly, "Yet we were wrong, terribly wrong. We owe it to future
generations to explain why."

The last room of the Museum is filled with images and symbols
of peace, and our guide explained, "The museum has a dual pur-
pose: to remember the war and to express the love of peace."
Here, Thompson and Colbourn were honored years before their
1998 recognition in their own country. Both are pictured and
praised for saving the lives of ten Vietnamese civilians at My Lai.
I had never heard of either man before my visit to this museum.

Similarly, I learned about Norman Morrison and Roger Laporte,
two of the eight Americans who immolated themselves to express
their opposition to the Vietnam War. Morrison immolated himself
outside of McNamara's office in the Pentagon on November 2,
1965. While his wife Anne was picking up their two school-aged

Peace tree in the War Remnants Museum.

children, Christina and Ben, Morrison drove over to the Pentagon with their one-year-old daughter Emily. While his act was generally ignored in the United States, it was revered in North Vietnam. In fact, NLF soldiers and their supporters heard the news of Morrison's suicide on their radios in Vietnam on November 2, and five days later North Vietnamese poet To Huu wrote a poem called "Emily My Child" that has since been studied by two generations of Vietnamese schoolchildren. A street was named in Morrison's honor in Hanoi.

In *In Retrospect*, McNamara did not write about what he saw through his window the afternoon of November 2, but he did write, "Morrison's death was a tragedy not only for his family but also for me and the country . . . Marg and our three children shared many of Morrison's feelings about the war . . . and I believed I understood and shared some of his thoughts."

Exactly one week after Morrison's death, Laporte sat down cross-legged in front of the United Nations Building in New York. On November 9, 1965, he died of self-inflicted burns during his protest of the American involvement in Vietnam.

The day after visiting the War Remnants Museum, I went to the Reunification Palace, now a museum open to the public. It had been the Independence Palace when it was constructed, and was commonly referred to as the Presidential Palace when occupied by Diem and then Thieu during the war years. Standing on the roof of the impressive structure that occupies an entire city block near the center of Ho Chi Minh City, looking over the grounds surrounded by a ten-foot-high fence, I had a much different view of the city than I had had as a young man driving by on my motorcycle.

Then, I had cast brief glances at the imposing edifice. But I never stopped to take a picture or even slowed down because we had been warned that the Palace guards were instructed to shoot anyone approaching the perimeter at any time of day. Standing on the helipad, looking toward the street in front of the building, I remembered a photo I had seen downstairs in the Palace of the first North Vietnamese tank breaking through the fence.

I struck up a conversation with a Vietnamese man standing near me and learned that he was about ten years younger than me and had been living in Saigon when the troops arrived from the North. He explained that in the morning, everyone stayed in their homes, afraid of what might happen as the soldiers rolled into the city. But after hearing on the radio that the President had resigned, some residents ventured out and found the troops celebrating, not shooting. Soon everyone poured out into the streets

Reunification Palace, Ho Chi Minh City, 2001. Currently a museum, formerly the Presidential Palace, which was the residence of South Vietnamese leaders from Ngo Dinh Diem in 1955 through Nguyen Van Thieu in 1975.

to join the celebration of the reunification of Vietnam over two decades after the partitioning that had occurred at Geneva in 1954. "We were happy," he explained, "because the war was over and we were no longer afraid of the North Vietnamese soldiers because they were not shooting because we were all Vietnamese." Hiding their uniforms, and wearing civilian clothes, even thousands of ARVN officers and enlisted men came out to celebrate.

Leaving the grounds later, I looked back and saw a different building than the one I had entered just hours earlier. What I had first perceived to be a nondescript façade functionally combining horizontal and vertical lines, I now realized corresponded to five significant Chinese characters representing good fortune, peace, democracy, prosperity, and power. Just another short lesson for me in how to see and understand another world.

There were many conspicuous changes in the city I had known as Saigon. The ubiquitous red flags of the ruling socialist party made clear how the war had ended. But the accompanying Coca-Cola umbrellas in front of every restaurant on every street countered that statement. Vietnamese describe the contemporary sociopolitical environment as "red capitalism."

Behind the conspicuous political and economic symbols, however, still lie some subtle, but significant examples of the dramatic cultural differences between the Vietnamese and the Americans. Sipping iced coffee one morning in a small neighborhood café adjacent to a tennis club, I watched the beginning of a lesson. A young boy walked out onto the clay court and bowed to his instructor. Although a basket of balls and rackets was at his side, the instructor simply faced the boy and moved slowly exactly where he was standing. He demonstrated to his student how to turn his shoulders, and bend his knees without moving his feet. It was a lesson in agility, not power.

Lessons

In a 1988 *60 Minutes* segment on the teaching of the history of the Vietnam War entitled "Vietnam 101," a young American college student notes, "It's not taught to us in high school." If it was, would the "lessons of Vietnam" be about the limits of American military power, or our misunderstandings of other nations and cultures, or the shackles placed upon the American military by our political leaders?

As early as 1970, former Secretary of Defense Clark Clifford articulated three lessons that he had learned after taking over from McNamara. In his essay, "Set a date in Vietnam. Stick to it. Get out," that appeared in the May 22 issue of *Life*, Clifford enumerated his lessons. "The national security of the U.S. is not involved in Vietnam, nor does our national interest in the area warrant our continued military presence there . . . We cannot win a military victory in South Vietnam, and we must, therefore, cease trying to do so . . . We cannot continue to fight the war in Vietnam without doing serious and irreparable injury to our own country."

The conclusion of *Hearts and Minds* explains, perhaps, why the lessons learned by Clifford were not mastered by his contemporaries. Recorded in 1974, the narrator's words resonate eerily today. "I think Americans have all tried very hard to escape what we learned in Vietnam."

In CBS's 1975 documentary *Vietnam: A War That Is Finished*, Walter Cronkite summed up the era: "We embarked on the path to Vietnam with good intentions, I think, but once upon the path we found ourselves having been misguided. Many of us, myself included, in our private personal opinions of the rightness of this course came half around. And perhaps that is our big lesson from Vietnam. The necessity for candor. We the American people—the world's most admired democracy—cannot ever again allow ourselves to be misinformed, manipulated and misled into disastrous foreign adventures. The government must share the big decisions with the people regarding the making of policy."

When Gerald Ford and Jimmy Carter were campaigning for the presidency in 1976, the Republican platform blamed a Democratic Congress for refusing to supply adequate military aid to South Vietnam and thus allowing the communists to win the war. Contrastingly, the Democratic Party platform asserted that the Vietnam War had taught us to avoid becoming militarily involved anywhere that our national interests are not at stake.

The narrator of "Legacies," the concluding episode to PBS's landmark Vietnam series, points out, "Vietnam can be viewed in retrospect as the longest of the post–World War II colonial conflicts. It can be viewed as a civil war. It can also be viewed as an episode of the Cold War like Korea in the 1950s. But whatever the view, it was a tragedy for the people of Vietnam, Cambodia and Laos. And the people of America." He eventually concludes,

Bicyclists in Hue riding to work on a spring morning in April 2001.

"America's Vietnam War is over, but it lives on in all those who experienced it. This and all future generations will have to turn to this long, dark and horrid chapter of history to define the meaning and determine the lessons of Vietnam."

McNamara subtitled *In Retrospect* "The Tragedy and Lessons of Vietnam," and his final chapter is "The Lessons of Vietnam." He lists and discusses eleven lessons. In a talk at Harvard in April 1995, the transcript of which is appended to McNamara's book, Professor Ernest May of the JFK School of Government suggested that McNamara's list could be consolidated into two ways of thinking about American policy:

> The first is . . . in thinking about any foreign area or any government or organized force in the world that has a different history and a different culture, we need to think about its history and culture and not assume that thought and behavior will be like ours. We have to think about people in their own contexts.
>
> The second is . . . when we think about doing something in the world, we should always very closely inspect our own premises. . . . [This] is a point of tremendous importance yet constantly forgotten.

May implies not only that the Americans did not understand the Vietnamese, but also that they misunderstood themselves as they committed the United States to fighting the longest war in its history fifty years ago.

Questions for Discussion

1. What effect did his year in Vietnam have on the author?
2. Why were the Paris Peace Talks that began in 1968 not concluded until 1973?
3. Why was the 1965 Gulf of Tonkin Resolution, which was passed so overwhelmingly by Congress, later repealed?
4. Why did the Nixon government oppose the publication of the Pentagon Papers?
5. Why did the U.S. Supreme Court rule in favor of the publication of the Pentagon Papers by the *New York Times* and the *Washington Post*?
6. What were the major effects of the war in Vietnam on the United States? What were its major effects on Vietnam?
7. What were the effects of the war on the surrounding countries of Laos, Cambodia, and Thailand?
8. What is the relationship between the United States and Vietnam today?
9. What are the similarities and dissimilarities between the Korean War and the Vietnam War?

Activities

1. Interview an American male friend, neighbor, or relative who served in Vietnam; interview an American male who was an adult during the war but did not serve in the military; interview an American female who was an adult during the war. Prepare a list of questions to elicit their perspectives at the beginning, during, and after the war. Learn what key events formed or changed their perspectives.

2. Interview a Vietnamese-American about his or her experiences or perspectives on the war.

3. Interview friends, neighbors, or relatives who were in high school in the 1970s, 1980s, 1990s, or the 2000s. Ask them what they learned about the war in their American History classes.

4. Read poems or short stories that deal with Vietnam. Read a novel or a work of nonfiction about American involvement in Vietnam.

5. Listen to music from the time of the war.

6. Watch a movie about a subject that is related to American involvement in Vietnam.

7. Study photographs of soldiers in Vietnam and Americans demonstrating in support of or opposition to the war.

Appendix A: American Troop Levels in Vietnam

1954–60—700 advisors

1961—3,000 advisors

1962—11,000 advisors

1963—16,300 advisors

1964—23,000 advisors

1965—184,300 advisors and combat troops

1966—389,000

1967—463,000

1968—495,000

April 1969—543,400

1969—428,400

1970—280,000

1971—156,800

1972—50,000

April 30, 1975—Last Americans, ten Marines, leave Saigon by helicopter from the roof of the U.S. Embassy

Appendix B: Casualties and Statistics

All numbers are estimates based on numerous sources

1,000,000—Vietnamese Catholics who moved to South Vietnam in 1954–1955

500,000—Vietnamese who moved to North Vietnam in 1954–1955

2,500,000—U.S. enlisted men who served in Vietnam (2 percent of those eligible for the draft); 80 percent were from working-class or poor families

58,202—Americans killed and named on the Vietnam Veterans' Memorial in Washington, D.C.

58,000—Vietnamese killed and named on the memorial at Cu Chi, one of hundreds of such memorials throughout Vietnam

304,704—Americans wounded

Over 5,000 soldiers killed and over 20,000 wounded from South Korea, Australia, Thailand, and New Zealand

2,338—American MIAs

766—American POWs

5,000—American draft resistors imprisoned

100,000—American Vietnam veteran suicides

70,000—Americans who went to Canada

1,000—American antiwar groups in 1973

223,748—ARVN soldiers killed

1,169,763—ARVN soldiers wounded

1,100,000—North Vietnamese and NLF soldiers killed

600,000—North Vietnamese and NLF soldiers wounded

Approximately 2,000,000—Vietnamese civilians killed

130,000—"Boat people" who fled Vietnam

65,000—Vietnamese evacuated by United States

130,000—Vietnamese who left following reunification

200,000—Vietnamese placed in re-education camps in Vietnam

Glossary

AID   Agency for International Development

ao dai   Traditional Vietnamese dress

ARVN   Army of the Republic of Vietnam (South Vietnam)

body count   Number of people killed

CIA   Central Intelligence Agency

DMZ   Demilitarized Zone

dong (also piasters)   Vietnamese currency

DRV   Democratic Republic of Vietnam (North Vietnam)

free fire zone   Area deemed completely under enemy control where American soldiers were free to fire at any nonallies

friendly fire   Ground or air fire mistakenly directed at friendly soldiers

gook   Derogatory term for any Vietnamese

green (or green money)   American currency; green dollars

grunt   Slang for American infantrymen

Huey   Nickname for the UH-1 helicopter

KIA   Killed in action

LZ   Landing zone (for helicopters)

MACV Military Assistance Command—Vietnam ("Mack vee"); United States command headquarters

MIA Missing in action

MPC Military Payment Certificates

NCO Noncommissioned officer

NFLSV National Front for the Liberation of South Vietnam; also NLF—National Liberation Front; also VC, Viet Cong

NVA North Vietnamese Army (PAVN)

OSS Office of Strategic Services (precursor of the CIA)

PAVN People's Army of Vietnam (North Vietnam)

piasters (also dong) Vietnamese currency

POW Prisoner of war

RVN Republic of Vietnam (South Vietnam)

sappers NVA and VC special assault soldiers

search and destroy Offensive operations conducted to find and kill enemy forces and their supplies rather than establish control of territory

Tet Vietnamese New Year celebration based on the lunar calendar

USIA United States Information Agency

U.S.S.R. Union of Soviet Socialist Republics

VC Viet Cong

VVAW Vietnam Veterans Against the War

WIA Wounded in action

Bibliography

Books

Appy, Christian G. *Patriots*. New York: Viking, 2003.

Bloodworth, Dennis. *An Eye for the Dragon*. New York: Farrar, Straus and Giroux, 1970.

Chong, Denise. *The Girl in the Picture*. New York: Viking, 1999.

Faas, Horst, and Tim Page, eds. *Requiem*. New York: Random House, 1997.

Fitzgerald, Frances. *Fire in the Lake*. New York: Random House, 1972.

Greene, Graham. *The Quiet American*. New York: Penguin, 1955.

Gutzman, Phillip. *Vietnam*. London: PRC Publishers, Ltd., 2002.

Hermann, Kenneth J., Jr. *Lepers and Lunacy: An American in Vietnam Today*. Author, 2003.

Ho Chi Minh. *The Prison Diary of Ho Chi Minh*. New York: Bantam Books, 1971.

Loewen, James. *Lies My Teacher Told Me*. New York: Touchstone Books, 1995.

McNamara, Robert S. *In Retrospect*. New York: Vintage Books, 1995.

Monuments and Sites in Commemoration of Uncle Ho and His Family in Hue. Hue, Vietnam: Thuan Hoa, 2001.

O'Brien, Tim. *The Things They Carried*. New York: Broadway Books, 1990.

Tang, Truong Nhu. *A Viet Cong Memoir*. New York: Vintage Books, 1986.

Veenis, William R., Jr. *Memorial*. Warren, PA: Jostens, 1984.

Articles

Clifford, Clark. "Set a date in Vietnam. Stick to it. Get out." *Life*, May 22, 1970.

Donovan, Hedley. "Winding Down the War on Our Own." *Life*, October 24, 1969.

Graham, Billy. "On Calley." *New York Times*, April 9, 1971.

Rostow, Walter W. "The Case for the Vietnam War." *Parameters: U.S. Army War College Quarterly*, winter 1996–97: 39–50.

Sack, John. "The True Story of M Company." *Esquire*, October 1966.

Videos

Cold War, Episode 14—"Vietnam"; and Episode 16—"Détente." CNN, 1998.

The Deer Hunter. Michael Cimino, 1978.

Hearts and Minds. Peter Davis, 1974.

Ho Chi Minh. Biography, A&E, 1998.

The Quiet American. Staffan Ahrenberg and William Horberg, 2002.

The Trials of Henry Kissinger. Alex Gibney and Eugene Jarecki, 2002.

"Vietnam 101." CBS, *60 Minutes*, 1988.

Vietnam: A Television History—"Roots of War," "The First Vietnam War," "America's Mandarin," "LBJ Goes to War," "America Takes Charge," "America's Enemy," "Tet 1968," "Vietnamizing the War," "Cambodia and Laos," "Peace Is at Hand," "Homefront USA," "The End of the Tunnel," and "Legacies." PBS—WGBH—1983.

Vietnam: A War That Is Finished. CBS, 1975.

Vietnam: In the Year of the Pig. Emile de Antonio, 1968.

Why Vietnam. U.S. Department of Defense, 1965.

Web Sites

Battlefield: Vietnam. http://www.pbs.org/battlefieldvietnam/.

Faces on the Wall. http://www.viethero.com.

History Channel. http://www.historychannel.com.

9th Med Lab. http://www.9thmedlab.org/.

Vets with a Mission. http://www.vwam.com.

"The Vietnam War," *The History Place*. http://www.historyplace.com/unitedstates/vietnam/index.html.

Index

About the Author

RUSSELL H. COWARD, JR. spent four years in the U.S. Air Force and taught English in Saigon, South Vietnam, during the Vietnam War. He currently directs the English Education program at the State University of New York, Brockport.